孔 孟 箴 言
Sayings of Confucius and Mencius

汉英对照读本

A Chinese – English Bilingual Textbook

李天辰　编译

Compiled and Translated by Li Tianchen

山东友谊出版社

Shandong Friendship Press

孔孟至言

Sayings of Confucius and Mencius

汉英对照读本

A Chinese-English bilingual text

刘士聪 编

Recorded and Translated by Liu Shicong

山东友谊出版社

Shandong Friendship Press

孔孟箴言

香港孔教學院

院長湯恩佳題

目　　录
Contents

前　言

　　孔子是中国古代伟大的思想家、政治家、教育家、儒家学派的创始人,是世界历史上最负盛名的人物之一。1984 年美国出版的《人民年鉴手册》把孔子列为世界十大思想家中的第一人。孟子也是中国古代伟大的思想家、教育家,是儒家学派的重要代表,孔子思想的主要继承人。历来孔孟思想并提,被誉为"孔孟之道"。饮誉中外的孔孟思想,在当时及日后两千多年的历史长河里发挥过积极作用。时至今日,其治国安邦之道,发展经济之道,社会管理之道等等,仍具有现实的社会价值。为弘扬中华民族优秀的传统文化并使之服务于现代社会,现将孔孟思想中的一些名言警句编写成《孔孟箴言》并译成现代汉语和英语,以供中外读者学习参考。

　　本书承蒙香港孔教学院院长汤恩佳先生赞助印行并亲自题写书名,不胜感激。汤先生多年来致力于弘扬孔学儒道,兴学术,倡教化,锲而不舍。谨以汤先生为楷模,在弘扬孔学儒道方面多做工作。在编译《孔孟箴言》过程中,得到了曲阜师范大学孔子文化学院骆承烈教授和山东师范大学外语学院刘世生教授的热情帮助,也在此一并表示感谢。

李天辰

1998 年 6 月于曲阜

Preface

Confucius (551 − 479 B. C.), the great thinker, statesman, educator, and the founder of the Confucian School of Thought in ancient China, is one of the supremely great figures in the world's history. He was listed in the first place among the world's ten great thinkers by 《The People's Almanac》which was published in America in 1984. Mencius is also a great thinker, educator, an important representative of the Confucian School of Thought in ancient China and the chief inheritor of Confucius' thoughts. All through the ages, the thoughts of Confucius and Mencius have been mentioned in the same breath and known as "the Doctrine of Confucius and Mencius". They have played a positive role in the Chinese history for over 2,000 years. Up to now , their thoughts on how to govern the country, how to develop economy and how to build an ideal society, are still of realistic significance. To help readers both at home and abroad acquire a better understanding of the thoughts of Confucius and Mencius, I compiled this booklet 《Sayings of Confucius and Mencius》and put it first from classical Chinese into modern Chinese and then into English.

I am greatly indebted to Mr. Tong Yun Kai, President of Hong Kong Confucian Academy, who sponsored the publication of the book and autographed the cover title. I am also greatly obliged to Professor Luo Chenglie of Qufu Teachers University and Professor Liu Shisheng of Shandong Teachers University, who offered me great help in the course of compiling and translation. My thanks are given to all those who have helped make the publication of this book possible.

June, 1998

Li Tianchen

为政篇第一

BOOK I TO GOVERN

孔子曰:"大道之行也,天下为公。选贤与能,讲信修睦。故人不独亲其亲,不独子其子;使老有所终,壮有所用,幼有所长,矜、寡、孤、独、废疾者、皆有所养;男有分,女有归。货,恶其弃于地也,不必藏于己;力,恶其不出于身也,不必为己。是故谋闭而不兴,盗窃乱贼而不作,故外户而不闭——是谓'大同'。"

(《礼记·礼运》)

〔译文〕孔子说:"大道推行之后,天下是大家的。选拔贤人举荐能人管理政治,人们之间讲求信义,提倡和睦。一个人不单以自己的亲人为亲人,不单以自己的儿子为儿子。人到老年有好的结局,壮年人有发挥能力的场所,幼年人能茁壮成长。那些老年无妻、无夫、无子,幼年无父母的,以及各种残疾人都能被收养。男人各有分工,女人均有归宿。把财货随便扔到地上被认为是可恶的,也不收归自己。人人为自己没有出力而不愉快,出了力也不为自己。于是,策划干坏事的人不干了,各种大盗小贼也没有了,各家的大门都不用关了。这样可谓是大同社会了。"

Confucius said, "In the ideal Society of Great Harmony, the world belongs to the public. The virtuous and competent are selected. Faithfulness is fostered and good neighbourliness is cultivated. People do not love their own parents or care for their own children. The aged will have their homes, the middle - aged will find their use and the youngsters are well bred. All solitary persons such as widows and widowers, the deformed and diseased, adults without children or children without parents, have a place to live in and are taken care of. All men have their positions, all women have each one's home. It is hateful to lay goods aside wastefully and unnecessary to hide it for oneself. It is also hateful to make no efforts of one's own and unnecessary to make efforts for oneself. Consequently, conspiracies are prevented, theft and robbery are stopped, and there is no need to shut the outer door of a house. This is the Society of Great Harmony."

子曰:"为政以德,譬如北辰,居其所而众星共之。"

（《论语·为政》）

〔译文〕孔子说:"治理国家时施行仁德,那么自己就如同天上的北极星一样,处在一定的位置上,而别的星辰都环绕着它。"

Confucius said, "He who rules by moral force is like the pole - star, which remains in its place while all the other stars surround it."

子曰:"道千乘之国,敬事而信,节用而爱人,使民以时。"

（《论语·学而》）

[译文]孔子说:"治理一个有千辆兵车的国家,对政事要严肃认真,信守诺言,节省费用,爱护百姓,使用百姓要在农闲的时候。"

Confucius said, "In ruling a state of one thousand war – chariots, the ruler should attend strictly to business, punctually observe his promises, economize in expenditure, show affection towards his subjects, and use labour of peasantry only in slack season of the year."

子曰:"道之以政,齐之以刑,民免而无耻;道之以德,齐之以礼,有耻且格。"

（《论语·为政》）

[译文]孔子说:"用政法来诱导他们,使用刑罚来整顿他们,人民只是暂时地免于罪过,却没有廉耻之心。如果用道德诱导他们,使用礼教来整顿他们,人民不但有廉耻之心,而且还会人心归服。"

Confucius said, "If you guide the people by regulations, keep order among them by punishments, they may avoid doing what is wrong, but they will also lose self-respect. If you guide the people by moral force, keep order among them by ritual, they will keep their self – respect, and come to you of their own accord."

　　孟子曰:"孔子曰:'道二,仁与不仁而已矣,'暴其民甚,则身弑国亡;不甚,则身危国削。"

　　　　　　　　　　　　　　　　　(《孟子·离娄上》)

　　[译文]孟子说:"孔子说:'治理国家的方法有两种,行仁政和不行仁政罢了。'如果对百姓很暴虐,自己就会被杀,国家就会灭亡。即使暴虐百姓不很厉害,自己本身也有危险,国力也会被削弱。"

　　Mencius said, "Confucius said, 'There are two ways in running a country , benevolent government and tyrannous government.' If one is tyrannous to the common people, he himself will be killed, the country is doomed; even if he is not very tyrannous, he is still in danger and the power of the country is weakened."

　　孟子曰:"尧舜之道,不以仁政,不能平治天下。"

　　　　　　　　　　　　　　　　　(《孟子·离娄上》)

　　[译文]孟子说:"即使有尧舜之道,如果不行仁政,也不能

治理好国家。"

Mencius said, "Even though the monarch has the principles of King Yao and King Shun, but if he is not benevolent, he can not run the country well."

孟子曰："地不改辟矣，民不改聚矣，行仁政而王，莫之能御也。"

（《孟子·公孙丑上》）

〔译文〕孟子说："国土不必再开拓，百姓不必再增加，只要实行仁政来统一天下，就没有人能够抵挡得了。"

Mencius said, "Land does not need opening up, nor does population need increasing. So long as the country is unified through benevolent government, it becomes unconquerable."

孟子曰："不仁而得国者，有之矣；不仁而得天下者，未之有也。"

（《孟子·尽心下》）

〔译文〕孟子说："不行仁道却能得到一个国家的事是有的。但不行仁道而能得到天下的事情，却未曾有过。"

Mencius said, "There are examples that an unbenevolent person can seize the power of a state, but there has been no example that an unbenevolent person can rule an empire."

孟子曰:"离娄之明,公输子之巧,不以规矩,不能成方圆;师旷之聪,不以六律,不能正五音;尧舜之道,不以仁政,不能平治天下。"

(《孟子·离娄上》)

〔译文〕孟子说:"既使有离娄那样明亮的视力,公输般那样灵巧的手艺,如果不用圆规和曲尺,也不能正确地画出方形和圆形。既使有著名乐师师旷的耳力,如果不用六律,便不能校正五音。既使有古代贤明帝王尧、舜的道,如果不行仁政,也不能管理好天下。"

Mencius said, "Even if one has such good eyesight as Li Lou, is so nimble-fingured as Gong Shuban, he can't draw a square or a circle without a pair of compasses or a crooked ruler. Even if one has the same hearing ability as the noted musician Shi Kuang, he can't correct the five notes without using the six rhythms. Even if one possesses the principles of the ancient sagacious kings as Yao and Shun, he can't run the country well without implementing benevolent government."

孟子曰:"君行仁政,斯民亲其上,死其长矣。"

（《孟子·梁惠王下》）

〔译文〕孟子曰:"您如果实行仁政,百姓自然会爱护他们的上级,甘愿为他们的长官牺牲了。"

Mencius said,"If the monarch is benevolent, the common people will naturally love their superiors and be willing to die for them. "

孟子曰:"三代之得天下也以仁,其失天下也以不仁。国之所以废兴存亡者亦然。天子不仁,不保四海;诸侯不仁,不保社稷;卿大夫不仁,不保宗庙;士庶人不仁,不保四体。今恶死亡而乐不仁,是犹恶醉而强酒。"

（《孟子·离娄上》）

〔译文〕孟子说:"夏、商、周三代帝王得到天下是因为行仁,他们的丧失天下是因为不行仁。一个国家的衰败和兴盛、存在和灭亡也是这个道理。天子如果不行仁,便不能保住他的天下;诸侯如果不行仁,便不能保住他的国家;卿大夫如果不行仁,便不能保住他们的祖庙;一般老百姓不行仁,便保不住自己的身体。现在有些人怕死却又喜欢不仁,这就好像怕醉酒却偏要喝酒一样。"

Mencius said,"The emperors of the Xia, Shang and Zhou

dynasties came into power because they implemented benevolence. Their descendants lost power because they did not implement benevolence. This truth applies to the rise and decline, existence and dying of a country. If an emperor does not implement benevolence, he can't keep his empire; a prince, his state; a minister, his ancestral temple; an ordinary person, his body. Now some people are afraid of death but unwilling to implement benevolence. This resembles the case that someone fears being drunk but forces himself to drink."

孟子曰:"……梁襄王卒然问曰:'天下恶乎定?'
吾对曰:'定于一。'
'孰能一之?'
对曰:'不嗜杀人者能一之。'
'孰能与之?'
对曰:'天下莫不与也。'"

(《孟子·梁惠王上》)

〔译文〕孟子说:"梁襄王突然问我:'天下要怎样才安定?'
我答道:'天下统一就会安定。'
他又问:'谁能统一天下呢?'
我又答:'不好杀人的国君能统一天下。'
他又问:'那有谁来跟随他呢?'
我又答:'天下的人没有不跟随他的。'"

Mencius said, "Duke Xiang of the Liang state Suddenly asked, 'Do you know how to make the country stable?'

I answered, 'so long as the country get unified.'

He asked again, 'Who can get the country unified?'

I answered, 'The monarch who is not addicted to slaughter.'

He went on asking, 'Who will follow him?'

I answered, 'All people in the world will follow him.'"

孟子曰:"以力服人者,非心服也,力不瞻也;以德服人者,中心悦而诚服也。"

(《孟子·公孙丑上》)

〔译文〕孟子说:"依仗实力来使人服从的,人家不会心悦诚服,只是因为人家力量不够才服从你;依靠道德来使人服从的,人家才会从心里高兴地真心实意地顺服你。"

Mencius said, "If you make others obedient by force, they are obedient because they can't match you, but they are never obedient at heart. However, if you make others obedient by virtue and morality, they will be obedient to you pleasantly and honestly."

孟子曰:"孔子曰:'仁不可为众也。夫国君好仁,天下无敌。'今也欲无敌于天下而不以仁，是犹执热而不以濯也。"

（《孟子·离娄上》）

〔译文〕孟子说："孔子说过：'仁的力量是不能以人数的多寡来衡量的。君主如果爱好仁，天下就不会有敌手。'如今一些诸侯要想天下无敌手，却又不去行仁，这好比一个人热得不得了，却又不肯洗澡一样。"

Mencius said, "Confucius said, 'The force of benevolence can not be measured with the number of people. If the emperor is fond of benevolence, he will be unconquerable all over the world.' Now some princes want to be unconquerable in the world, but do not implement benevolence. That's just as if someone feels extremely hot but is unwilling to take a bath."

孟子曰："尽信《书》，则不如无《书》，吾于《武成》取二三策而已矣。仁人无敌于天下，以至仁伐至不仁，而何其血之流杵也？"

（《孟子·尽心下》）

〔译文〕孟子说："完全相信《尚书》，不如没有《尚书》。我对于《尚书》中的《武成》篇，不过取两三页罢了。仁人在天下没有敌手。以周武王这么仁道的人去讨伐商纣王那种极不仁道的人，怎么会使血流得连捣米的杵也漂起来呢？"

Mencius said, "I would rather not possess The Book of History than believe it completely. I have used only two or three pages from the article "Wu Cheng" in the book. Benevolent people are unconquerable all over the world. When the most benevolent King Wu of the Zhou dynasty sent a punitive expedition against the extremely unbenevolent and virtueless King Zhou of the Shang dynasty, how could it be so bleeding that pestles were floated?"

孟子曰:"庖有肥肉,厩有肥马,民有饥色,野有饿莩,此率兽而食人也。兽相食,且人恶之;为民父母,行政,不免于率兽而食人,恶在其为民父母也?"

(《孟子·梁惠王上》)

〔译文〕孟子说:"现在你的厨房里有肥肉,马厩里有肥马,可是老百姓却面带饥色,野外躺着饿死的尸体,这就等于在上位的人率领禽兽来吃人。兽类自相残杀,人们尚且厌恶,做百姓父母官的人主持政务时,却不免于率领禽兽来吃人,那又怎么能做老百姓的父母官呢?"

Mencius said, "You have fat meat in the kitchen and fat horses in the stable, but the common people look hungry and there are starved corpses outside. This is just as if the superiors bring wild beasts to eat the common people. Wild beasts kill each other, at which people are disgusted. How can those people in office possibly be good government officials if they will bring wild beasts to eat the common people?"

孟子曰:"是以惟仁者宜在高位。不仁而在高位,是播其恶于众也。"

(《孟子·离娄上》)

〔译文〕孟子说:"只有道德高尚的仁人,才应该处于统治地位。如果道德低下的不仁之人处于统治地位,就会把他的恶行传播给群众。"

Mencius said, "Only those benevolent and virtuous people should be in the ruling position. If the unbenevolent and virtueless people are in the ruling position, they will spread their evil doings among the common people."

孟子曰:"人不足与适也,政不足闲也;唯大人为能格君心之非。君仁,莫不仁;君义,莫不义;君正,莫不正。一正君而国定矣。"

(《孟子·离娄上》)

〔译文〕孟子说:"那些当政的小人不值得去谴责,他们的施政也不值得去非议;只有大人才能纠正国君的不正确思想。国君行仁,便没有人不仁;国君守义,便没有人不义。国君正,便没有人不正,一旦把国君端正,国家也就安定了。"

Mencius said, "Those petty men in office aren't worth our criticism , nor is their administration worth our reproaching. Only great men can correct the monarch's wrong ideas. If the monarch implements benevolence, no one doesn't. If the monarch adheres to justice, no one doesn't, either. And if the monarch is upright, no one is not upright. Once the monarch is correct and upright, the country becomes stable. "

孟子曰:"仁则荣,不仁则辱;今恶辱而居不仁,是犹恶湿而居下也。如恶之,莫如贵德而尊士,贤者在位,能者在职;国家闲暇,及是时,明其政刑。唯大国,必畏之矣。"

(《孟子·公孙丑上》)

〔译文〕孟子说:"当权者如果行仁,就会有荣耀;如果不行仁,就会遭受屈辱。现在有的人非常厌恶屈辱却又不行仁,这好比厌恶潮湿却又处于低洼地方一样。如果真正厌恶屈辱,最好是以德为贵并尊敬士人,使有德行的人当政,使有能力的人担任一定职务;国家无内忧外患,趁这个机会,修政令,明法典,纵使强大的邻国也一定会畏惧了。"

Mencius said, "If those who are in power are benevolent, they will enjoy glory. If they are not benevolent, they will suffer humiliation. Some detest humiliation but do not try to be benevolent. This is just like being disgusted with humidity but still living in a low-lying ground. If they really detest humiliation, the best thing for them to do is to highly value morality, respect scholars, let the virtuous in power, and let the competent hold certain posts. In this way, the country will suffer no domestic trouble and foreign invasion. The authorities should take advantage of the occasion to make clear and definite the policies and laws. This being the case, even the powerful neighbouring countries will be awestricken. "

　　孟子见梁惠王。王曰:"叟! 不远千里而来,亦将有以利吾国乎?"

　　孟子对曰:"王! 何必曰利? 亦有仁义而已矣。……苟为后义而先利,不夺不餍。未有仁而遗其亲者也,未有义而后其君者也。王亦曰仁义而已矣,何必曰利?"

(《孟子·梁惠王上》)

　　〔译文〕孟子谒见梁惠王。惠王说:"老先生! 您不辞辛苦千里迢迢地到我们这里来,是不是要给我们国家带来什么利益呢?"

　　孟子回答道:"王,您为什么开口就讲利呢? 只要讲仁义就行了。……假若轻公义,重私利,那大夫若不把国君的产业夺去,是永远不会满足的。从来没见过讲仁却又遗弃自己父母的人,也没有见过讲义却又怠慢自己君主的人。王也只讲仁义就行了,为什么定要讲利呢?"

Mencius visited Duke Hui of the Liang State. The duke said, "Old man , you went to the trouble of travelling a long distance to come here. What benefits have you brought to our state?"

Mencius answered, "Your Highness, why do you talk about benefits first? It's all right to talk about benevolence and justice. ···If a senior official puts justice behind private benefits, he would never be satisfied till he has seized the monarch's property. There is no example that a benevolent man would abandon his parents, nor example that a just man would neglect his monarch. It is good if your Highness merely talk about benevolence and justice. Why do you only talk about benefits?"

孟子曰:"得百里之地而君之,皆能以朝诸侯,有天下。行一不义,杀一不辜,而得天下,皆不为也。是则同。"

(《孟子·公孙丑上》)

〔译文〕孟子说:"如果得到纵横各一百里的土地,而以他们为君王,他们都能使诸侯来朝觐,统一天下。如果让他们做一件不合道理的事,杀一个没有犯罪的人,因而得到天下,他们都不会做的。这是他们相同的地方。"

Mencius said, "If they are appointed monarch of a country of one hundred square li, they can deal well with the dukes and get the world unified. But if they are asked to do an unjust thing or to kill an innocent person so as to obtain the world, none of them will do this. this is where they are alike."

子贡问政。子曰:"足食,足兵,民信之矣。"

子贡曰:"必不得已而去,于斯三者何先?"曰:"去兵。"

子贡曰:"必不得已而去,于斯二者何先?"曰:"去食。自古皆有死,民无信不立。"

(《论语·颜渊》)

〔译文〕子贡问怎样治理政事。孔子说:"粮食充足,军备充足,人民信任政府。"子贡说:"如果迫不得已一定要去掉一项,在这三项中先去掉哪一项?"孔子说:"去掉军备。"子贡说:"如果迫不得已还要去掉一项,在这两项中先去掉哪一项?"孔子说:"去掉粮食。自古以来,人都会死,失去人民的信任,国家就站不住了。"

Zi Gong asked about the essentials of good government. Confucius said, "Sufficient food, sufficient armies and weapons, and the confidence of the common people." Zi Gong said. "Suppose you had no choice but to dispense with one of these three, which would you forgo first?" Confucius said, "Armies and weapons." Zi Gong said, "Suppose you were forced to dispense with one of the two that were left, which would you forgo?" Confucius said, "Food. Men have always been subject to death ever since, but without the confidence of the people there would be no government."

孔子曰："老者安之,朋友信之,少者怀之。"

(《论语·公冶长》)

〔译文〕孔子说："我的志向是:使老人得到安逸,朋友们信得过我,年青人怀念我。"

Confucius said, "My aspiration is that the aged live an easy life, friends have faith in me and the youth cherish the memory of me."

孟子曰："民为贵,社稷次之,君为轻。"

(《孟子·尽心下》)

〔译文〕孟子说："百姓最为重要,代表国家的土谷之神次之,君主最轻。"

Mencius said, " The common people are of the greatest importance, the country comes the second, the monarch comes the last."

　　孟子曰："桀纣之失天下也,失其民也;失其民者,失其心也。得天下有道:得其民,斯得天下矣;得其民有道:得其心,斯得民矣;得其心有道:所欲与之聚之,所恶勿施,尔也。"

(《孟子·离娄上》)

　　〔译文〕孟子说:"桀和纣丧失天下,是因为他们失去了百姓的支持;他们失去百姓的支持,是因为失去了民心。要想得到天下有办法,那就是必须得到百姓的支持,得到百姓的支持便能得到天下;要想得到百姓的支持也有办法,那就是必须得民心,得到了民心便得到了百姓的支持;要想得到民心,也有办法:那就是百姓喜欢的,给他聚集起来,他们不喜欢的,不要强加到他们头上,如此而已。"

　　Mencius said, "Emperor Jie and Emperor Zhou lost power because they didn't enjoy people's support. They didn't enjoy people's support because they lost their trust. The way to obtain the world is to get people's support: the way to obtain people's support is to obtain their trust: the way to obtain people's trust is to collect and give them what they want, but never do to them what they do not want. That's all there is to it!"

　　齐宣王问曰:"德何如则可以王矣?"
　　孟子答曰:"保民而王,莫之能御也。"

(《孟子·梁惠王上》)

〔译文〕宣王问道:"要有怎样的品行才能够统一天下呢?"

孟子回答说:"尽一切努力使老百姓的生活安定,这样去统一天下,就没有人能阻挡得了。"

Duke Xuan of the Qi State asked, "To unify the country, what kind of moral integrity should I have?"

Mencius answered, "Make your people's life as stable as you can, then nobody can prevent you."

滕文公问为国。

孟子曰:"民事不可缓也。"

(《孟子·滕文公上》)

〔译文〕滕文公向孟子问怎样治理国家的事情。

孟子说:"关心人民是最为紧迫的任务。"

Duke Wen of the Teng State asked about how to run a country.

Mencius said, "To care for the people is the most urgent task."

孟子曰:"禹思天下有溺者,由己溺之也;稷思天下有饥者,由己饥之也,是以如是其急也。"

（《孟子·离娄下》）

〔译文〕孟子曰："禹想到天下有人被水淹没，就好像自己使他们被淹没一样；稷想到天下有人在挨饿，就好像自己使他们挨饿一样，所以他们拯救百姓才这样急迫。"

Mencius said, "King Yu thought of someone in the world drowning, as if he himself put him to the position. King Ji thought of someone in the world suffering hunger, as if he himself put him to the position. So they were so eager to save the common people."

孟子曰："……是故明君制民之产，必使仰足以事父母，俯足以畜妻子，乐岁终身饱，凶年免于死亡；然后驱而之善，故民之从之也轻。"

（《孟子·梁惠王上》）

〔译文〕孟子说："……所以说贤明的君主在规定百姓的产业时，一定要使他们上足以养父母，下足以养妻子儿女，遇上好年成，能丰衣足食，遇上坏年成，也不至于饿死。然后再教导他们走上善的道路，他们也就很自然地听从了。"

Mencius said, "Therefore, when a wise monarch draws up the property policy, he must enable the people to support their parents and feed their wives and children, have ample food and clothing in good harvest years and be not starved to death in years of famine. Then when he instructs his people to take the virtuous road, they will naturally obey and follow."

孟子曰:"不违农时,谷不可胜食也;数罟不入洿池,鱼鳖不可胜食也;斧斤以时入山林,材木不可胜用也。谷与鱼鳖不可胜食,材木不可胜用,是使民养生丧死无憾也。养生丧死无憾,王道之始也。"

(《孟子·梁惠王上》)

〔译文〕孟子说:"如果不在农民耕种收获的季节,去征发他们干事,生产的粮食便吃不尽。如果不持细密的鱼网到大池中捕鱼,那么鱼类便吃不完。如果依照合适的时间到山林砍伐树木,木材也用不尽。粮食和鱼类吃不完,木材用不尽,这样便会使百姓对生养死葬都没有什么不满。百姓对生养死葬都满意,王道便开始了。"

Mencius said, "If the peasants aren't called up for corvee in sowing and harvesting seasons, they will produce sufficient grain; if one does not use fine and closely woven nets te catch fish in big pools, there will be plenty of it; if trees in the forest are felled at proper times, timber will never be used up. When grain, fish and timber are sufficient, the common people aren't worried about life and death. And consequently the Kingly way prevails."

孟子曰:"乐民之乐者,民亦乐其乐;忧民之忧者,民亦忧其忧。乐以天下,忧以天下,然而不王者,未之有也。"

(《孟子·梁惠王下》)

[译文]孟子曰:"以百姓的快乐为自己的快乐,百姓也会以你的快乐为自己的快乐;以百姓的忧愁为自己的忧愁,百姓也会以你的忧愁为自己的忧愁。如果和天下的人同忧同乐,还不能使天下人归附,那是从来没有的事。"

Mencius said, "If a monarch regards the happiness and worries of the common people as his own , they will regard his happiness and worries as theirs. And if the people under heaven share happiness and worries with him, there is no such case in which they don't submit to his authority."

孟子曰:"以佚道使民,虽劳不怨。以生道杀民,虽死不怨杀者。"

(《孟子·尽心上》)

[译文]孟子说:"在保证百姓安逸的情况下来役使百姓,百姓虽然劳苦,也不怨恨。在谋求百姓生存的原则下来杀人,那个人虽被杀死,也不会怨恨杀他的人。"

Mencius said, "If the common people are made to work in their spare time, though they toil, they never resent it. If a man is killed for the sake of saving the people, he is not resentful of the killer."

孟子曰:"以善服人者,未有能服人者也;以善养人,然后能服天下。天下不心服而王者,未之有也。"

(《孟子·离娄下》)

〔译文〕孟子说:"用善行来使人服从,没有能够使人服从的;用善来薰陶教养人,才能使天下的人归服你。天下人不心服却能统一天下的事,是从来没有的。"

Mencius said, "There is no one who can make others obedient by his good behaviours. But one can make the people under heaven obedient by educating and edifying them. One can never get the country unified when the people aren't obedient at heart."

孟子曰:"天时不如地利,地利不如人和。三里之城,七里之郭,环而攻之而不胜。夫环而攻之,必有得天时者矣;然而不胜者,是天时不如地利也。城非不高也,池非不深也,兵革非不坚利也,米粟非不多也;委而去之,是地利不如人和也。"

(《孟子·公孙丑下》)

[译文]孟子说:"天时不如地利,地利不如人和。比方有一座周边三里、外部仅有七里的小城,敌人围攻它却不能取胜。在长期围攻中,一定有合乎天时的战机,不能战胜,这就是说得天时的不如占地利的。城墙不是不高,护城河不是不深,兵器和甲胄不是不坚固锐利,粮食不是不多,然而敌人一来便弃城逃走,这就是说占地利的不如得人和的。

Mencius said, "Timeliness is inferior to topographical advantages which is in turn next to the support of the people. For instance, there is a city which is three li in circumference, the outskirt of which is seven li in circumference. The enemy troops encircle it but can't take it. During the long term of encirclement, there must be an opportunity, but they can't win. This is because timeliness isn't as important as topographical advantages. The city wall is high, the water in the city moat is deep, weapons and armour are sharp and sturdy, and grains are sufficient. But the city is given up as soon as enemy troops come." "This is because topographical advantages are not so important as the people's support."

孟子曰:"……得道者多助,失道者寡助。寡助之至,亲戚畔之;多助之至,天下顺之。以天下之所顺,攻亲戚之所畔;故君子有不战,战必胜矣。"

(《孟子·公孙丑下》)

〔译文〕孟子说:"……行仁政的帮助他的人就多,不行仁政的帮助他的人就少。帮助者少的时候,甚至连亲戚都背叛他;帮助者多的时候,全天下人都顺从他。拿全天下顺从的力量,攻打连亲戚都反对的人;那么,仁君圣主或者不用战争,若用战争,是必然胜利的了。"

Mencius said, "He who implements benevolence enjoys abundant support. All people under heaven are obedient to him. But he who does not implement benevolence enjoys little support. Even his relatives are against him. If the man who implements benevolence fights the man who does not, he is sure to win."

孟子曰:"天下信之,东面而征,西夷怨;南面而征,北狄怨。曰'奚为后我?'民望之,若大旱之望云霓也。"

（《孟子·梁惠王下》）

〔译文〕孟子说:"(商汤因为行仁,所以)天下人都很信任他,所以他向东方进军,西方国家的百姓便不高兴;他向南方进军,北方国家的百姓便不高兴。他们都说'为什么把我们放到后面呢?'人们盼望他,就好像久旱盼望乌云和虹霓一样。"

Mencius said, "The poeple under heaven trusted Emperor Tang of the Shang dynasty because of his benevolent government. When he marched to the east, people in the western states were not pleased. When he marched to the south, people in the northern states were not pleased. They all said, 'Why leave us behind?' People were looking forward to his coming as if they were expecting clouds and rainbows in dry weather."

孟子曰:"尊贤使能,俊杰在位,则天下之士皆悦,而愿立于其朝矣。"

(《孟子·公孙丑上》)

〔译文〕孟子说:"尊重贤才,使用能人,使杰出的人物都能居于官位,那么天下的士子都会很高兴,愿意到朝廷里去做事了。"

Mencius said, "If the court respects the able and virtuous persons, employs the competent, and let the outstanding persons hold official positions, then all the scholars of the country will be glad and willing to serve in the court."

哀公问曰:"何为则民服?"孔子对曰:"举直错诸枉,则民服;举枉错诸直,则民不服。"

(《论语·为政》)

〔译文〕鲁哀公问道:"怎样做才能使老百姓服从呢?"孔子回答说:"把正直的人提拔起来,放在邪曲的人上面,老百姓就会服从;如果把邪曲的人提拔起来,放在正直的人上面,老百姓就不会服从。"

Duke Ai asked, "What shall I do that the common people may be submissive?" Confucius said, "If you promote the straight and set them on top of the crooked, they will be submissive; if you promote the crooked and set them on top of the straight, they will not be submissive."

仲弓为季氏宰,问政。子曰:"先有司,赦小过,举贤才。"曰:"焉知贤才而举之?"子曰:"举尔所知;尔所不知,人其舍诸?"

(《论语·子路》)

〔译文〕仲弓做了季氏的家臣,向孔子请教怎样管理政事。孔子说:"给工作人员带头,不计较人家的小错误,提拔优秀人才。"仲弓说:"怎样去识别优秀人才把他们提拔出来呢?"孔子说:"提拔你所知道的;那些你所不知道的,别人难道会埋没他们吗?"

Zhong Gong, having become the steward of the Ji family, asked about governing. Confucius said, "You must take a lead for your subordinates, forgive their minor mistakes, and promote men of superior capacity."

Zhong Gong again asked, "How shall I recognize the men of superior capacity, in order to promote them?" Confucius said, "Promote those you know to be such. And how will others neglect those you do not know?"

孟子曰:"不信仁贤,则国空虚;无礼义,则上下乱;无政事,则财用不足。"

(《孟子·尽心下》)

〔译文〕孟子说:"不信任仁德贤能的人,国家就会空虚;没有礼义,上下的关系就会混乱;没有好的政事,国家的钱财就会不够用。"

Mencius said, "If the authorities do not trust the benevolent and virtuous people, the state will be actually vacant. Without rites and justice, there will be disorder in the relations between the high and the low. Without good political affairs, the state will not have enough wealth for use."

孟子曰:"虞不用百里奚而亡,秦穆公用之而霸。不用贤则亡,削何可得与?"

(《孟子·告子下》)

〔译文〕孟子说:"虞国不用百里奚因而灭亡,秦穆公用了百里奚因而称霸。不用贤人就会遭到灭亡,即使要求勉强存在,也是办不到的。"

Mencius said, "The Yu State was destroyed because of not appointing Baili Xi, while Duke Mu of the Qin State acted like an overlord because he appointed Baili Xi. Not appointing the able and virtuous will lead a state to destruction. It is even not possible to have an inadequate existance.

孟子曰:"国君进贤,如不得已,将使卑逾尊,疏逾戚,可不慎与? 左右皆曰贤,未可也;诸大夫皆曰贤,未可也;国人皆曰贤,然后察之;见贤焉,然后用之。左右皆曰不可,勿听;诸大夫皆曰不可,勿听;国人皆曰不可,然后察之;见不可焉,然后去之。左右皆曰可杀,勿听;诸大夫皆曰可杀,勿听;国人皆曰可杀,然后察之;见可杀焉,然后杀之。故曰,国人杀之也。如此,然后可以为民父母。"

(《孟子·梁惠王下》)

〔译文〕孟子说:"国君选拔贤人时,如果迫不得已,可以把卑贱者提拔到尊贵者之上,把疏远的人提拔到亲近的人之上,对这样的事能不慎重吗? 左右亲近的人都说某人好,不可轻信;众大夫都说某人好,也不可轻信;全国人都说某人好,然后去了解,发现他真有才干,再任用他。左右亲近的人都说某人不好,不可轻信;众大夫都说某人不好,也不可轻信;全国人都说某人不好,然后去了解,发现他真的不好,再罢免他。左右亲近的人都说某人该杀,不可轻信;众大夫都说某人该杀,也不可轻信;全国人都说某人该杀,然后去了解,发现他真的该杀,再杀他。所以说,这是全国人杀的。这样,才可以做百姓的父母。"

Mencius said, "When the monarch selects the able and virtuous people, if he has no other alternative, he may put the lowly higher than the honourable and the estranged higher than the intimate. Couldn't he be prudent in dealing with such matters? Although his intimate attendents all say that somebody is good, he should not readily believe. Although the senior officials all say that somebody is good, he should not readily believe either. When people all over the country say that somebody is good, then he can go and find the case. On finding that the person in question really has abilities, he can put this person in office. Although his intimate attendents all say that somebody is not good, he should not readily believe. Although the senior officials all say that somebody is not good, he should not readily believe either. When all the people in the country say that somebody is not good, then he can go and find the case. On finding that the person in question is really not good, he can dismiss him from office. Although his intimate attendents all say that somebody should be killed, he should not readily believe. Although the senior officials all say that somebody should be killed , he should not readily believe either. When people all over the country say that somebody should be killed, then he can go and find the case. On finding that the person in question really deserves the death penalty, he can sentence this person to death. So it can be said that this person is killed by all the people in the country. Only in this way , can the monarch be the common people's parent."

孟子曰："悦贤不能举,又不能养也,可谓悦贤乎?"

(《孟子·万章下》)

〔译文〕孟子说:"喜欢贤人,却不能重用,又不能照顾他的生活,能说是喜欢贤人吗?"

Mencius said, "If one likes the able and virtuous people but fails to promote and take care of them, how can we say that he really likes the able and virtuous?"

陈子曰:"古之君子何如则仕?"

孟子曰:"所就三,所去三。迎之致敬以有礼;言,将行其言也,则就之。礼貌未衰,言弗行也,则去之。其次,虽未行其言也,迎之致敬以有礼,则就之。礼貌衰,则去之。"

(《孟子·告子下》)

〔译文〕陈子问:"古时的君子在什么情况下才出来做官

呢?"

孟子回答说:"有三种情况可以就职,也有三种情况可以离职。很恭敬礼貌地迎接他;打算按他说的办,便就职。礼貌虽然没有减少,但是不按他说的办,便离开。其次,虽然没有按他说的话办事,但是很礼貌很恭敬地迎接他,便就职。礼貌减少了,便离去。"

Chen Zi asked, "What was the proper time for the gentleman in ancient times to go out and assume office?"

Mencius answered, "There were three situations for the gentleman to assume office and there were also three situations for him to leave office. If the authorities received him according to the tries and was going to do according to his advice, he would assume office. If the rites were not reduced but the monarch did not act according to his advice, he would leave office. Next, although the authorities did not act according to his opinion but welcomed him very politely and respectfully, he could assume office. If the rites were reduced, he would leave office."

孟子曰:"禹恶旨酒而好善言。汤执中,立贤无方。文王视民如伤,望道而未之见。武王不泄迩,不忘远。周公思兼三王,以施四事;其有不合者,仰而思之,夜以继日;幸而得之,坐以待旦。"

(《孟子·离娄下》)

〔译文〕孟子说:"禹不喜欢美酒,却喜欢有价值的话。汤持中正之道,举拔贤人却不拘泥于常规。文王疼爱百姓,好像他们受了伤害一样,寻求道理又似乎没看见一样。武王不轻侮周围的近臣,不忘记四方的远臣。周公要兼学夏、商、周三代君王,来实践禹、汤、文王、武王的勋业;如有与情况不合的,则抬头考虑,日夜不停地在想;侥幸想通了,便坐着等到天明立即去办。"

Mencius said, "King Yu didn't like fine wine, but he liked valuable words. King Tang adhered to the correct and upright way, selected and promoted men of virtue without following outmoded conventions. King Wen loved the common people as if they were hurt. He sought truth and was never conceited. King Wu showed loving care for the officials around him and never neglected those remote from him. King Zhou wanted to learn from the three sage kings of the Xia, Shang and Zhou dynasties so as to realize the great achievements of kings Yu, Tang, Wen and Wu. If there was something contradictory, he would look up and think of it day and night. When he straightened out his thinking, he sat up till daybreak and then did it at once."

孟子曰:"入其疆,土地辟,田野治,养老尊贤,俊杰在位,则有庆;庆以地。入其疆,土地荒芜,遗老失贤,掊克在位,则有让。"

(《孟子·告子下》)

[译文]孟子说:"进入某国的疆界后,如果看到土地已经开辟,田野里的工作也搞得很好,老人被赡养,贤者受尊重,杰出的人物都各居其位,就要有赏赐;赏赐给土地。如果一进入某国的疆界,看到的是土地荒废,老人被遗弃,贤者不被任用,善于搜刮钱财的人却立于朝廷,那就应该惩罚。"

Mencius said, "After entering the boundary of a certain state, if the monarch sees that the land is cultivated, the work in the field is done well, the old are supported, the virtuous are respected, and the outstanding all hold their posts, he should grant rewards, that is, rewarding people with lands. If he sees that the land lies waste, the old are abandoned, the virtuous persons are not appointed, but those who are good at extorting money from the people hold posts at the royal court, then he should give punishments."

孟子曰:"言无实不祥。不祥之实,蔽贤者当之。"
(《孟子·离娄下》)

[译文]孟子说:"说话而无内容,无作用,是不好的。这种不好的结果,将由那些妨碍进用贤才的人来承担。"

Mencius said, "It is not good to make empty and useless

talks. Let those who hinder the recommendation of the able and virtuous persons bear such kind of bad results."

季康子问政于孔子。孔子对曰:"政者,正也。子帅以正,孰敢不正?"

(《论语·颜渊》)

〔译文〕季康子问孔子怎样治理政事。孔子回答说:"政就是端正的意思。您带头走正路,谁敢不走正路呢?"

Ji Kangzi asked about government. Confucius said, "To govern is to keep straight. If you take a lead in doing so, who will dare to act otherwise?"

子曰:"其身正,不令而行;其身不正,虽令不从。"

(《论语·子路》)

〔译文〕孔子说:"如果本身行为正当,不用发令,别人也会照你的样子干;如果自己行为不正,虽然发号施令,却没有人听从你的。"

Confucius said, "If the ruler is personally upright, all will do well even though he does not give orders. But if he is not personally upright, even though he gives orders, they will not be obedient."

子曰:"苟正其身矣,于从政乎何有? 不能正其身,如正人何?"

(《论语·颜渊》)

[译文]孔子说:"如果统治者能够端正自己,管理政事还有什么困难? 如果不能端正自己,又怎么能端正别人呢?"

Confucius said, "If a ruler has rendered himself correct, he will have no trouble governing. If he can not render himself correct, how can he correct others?"

子曰:"上好礼,则民易使也。"

(《论语·宪问》)

[译文]孔子说:"在上位的人若遇事依礼而行,那么百姓就容易听从指挥。"

Confucius said, "If those at the top act on rites, the people are easy to direct."

季康子患盗,问于孔子。孔子对曰:"苟子之不欲,虽赏之不窃。"

(《论语·颜渊》)

〔译文〕季康子忧患盗贼太多,问孔子怎么办。孔子回答说:"如果你不贪求太多的话,那怕是奖励偷窃,也没人会去干的。"

Ji Kangzi, being vexed by robbers, asked Confucius for advice. Confucius replied, "If you can check your own cupidity, there will be no stealing, even though rewards should be offered for theft."

季康子问:"使民敬、忠以劝,如之何?"子曰:"临之以庄,则敬;孝慈,则忠;举善而教不能,则劝。"

(《论语·为政》)

〔译文〕季康子问:"要使老百姓恭敬、忠心和互相劝勉为善,应该怎么办呢?"孔子说:"你对待他们态度庄重,他们就会恭敬;你孝敬父母、慈爱百姓,他们就会忠心;你举荐好人,教育能力差的人,他们就会劝勉。"

Ji kangzi asked how to get the common people to be respectful and loyal and encourage each other. Confucius said, "Approach them with dignity, they will respect you. Show piety towards your parents and kindness towards the common people, they will be loyal to you. Promote those who are worthy, train those who are incompetent, they will encourage each other in behaving well."

孟子告齐宣王曰:"君之视臣如手足,则臣视君如腹心;君之视臣如犬马,则臣视君如国人;君之视臣如土芥,则臣视君如寇仇。"

(《孟子·离娄下》)

[译文]孟子告诉齐宣王说:"如果君主把臣下看成自己的手足,臣下就会把君主当作腹心;如果君主把臣下看成牛马,臣下就会把君主当作一般人;如果君主把臣下看成泥土或野草,臣下就会把君主看作仇敌。"

Mencius said to Duke Xuan of the Qi State, "If the monarch regards his subjects as his own hands and feet, they will regard him as their bellies and hearts; if the monarch regards his subjects as cattle and horse they will regard him as a passer－by; if the monarch regards his subjects as clay or wild weeds, they will regard him as an enemy."

子张问于孔子曰:"何如斯可以从政矣?"
子曰:"尊五美,屏四恶,斯可以从政矣。"
子张曰:"何谓五美?"

子曰:"君子惠而不费,劳而不怨,欲而不贪,泰而不骄,威而不猛。"

子张曰:"何谓惠而不费?"

子曰:"因民之所利而利之,斯不亦惠而不费乎? 择可劳而劳之,又谁怨? 欲仁而得仁,又焉贪? 君子无众寡,无小大,无敢慢,斯不亦泰而不骄乎? 君子正其衣冠,尊其瞻视,俨然人望而畏之,斯不亦威而不猛乎?"

子张曰:"何谓四恶?"

子曰:"不教而杀谓之虐,不戒视成谓之暴,慢令致期谓之贼,犹之与人也出纳之吝谓之有司。"

(《论语·尧曰》)

〔译文〕子张问孔子说:"怎样才能治理政事呢?"

孔子说:"尊重五种美德,屏弃四种被人厌恶的毛病,就可以治理政事了。"

子张说:"五种美德是什么呢?"

孔子说:"君子使老百姓得到好处,却不浪费;使唤老百姓,而老百姓却不怨恨;追求仁义,而不贪图财利;性情安泰,而不骄傲;态度威严,而不凶猛。"

子张说:"使老百姓得到好处,却不浪费应该怎么办呢?"

孔子说:"老百姓所应得到的好处就让他们得到它,这不就是使老百姓得到好处而不浪费吗? 选择老百姓可以干的事情而叫他们去干,还有谁会怨恨呢? 追求仁义而得到了仁义,还贪图什么呢? 无论人多人少,无论势力大小,君子都不敢怠慢,这不就是安泰而不骄傲吗? 君子衣冠整齐,目不斜视,态度庄重,使人望见而生敬畏之心,这不就是威严而不凶猛吗?"

子张说:"四种被人厌恶的毛病是什么呢?"

孔子说:"不先进行教育,而他们犯了罪便加杀戮,叫做虐;不事先告诫而要求立即成功,叫做暴;下达可以缓慢执行的政令而改为限期完成,叫做贼;该给人家的财物而舍不得拿出去,叫做小家子气。"

Zi Zhang asked Confucius, "What must be done to prepare oneself for service in the government?"

Confucius said, "Esteem the five fine qualities, and avoid the four evils, then you can serve in the government."

Zi Zhang asked, "What are the five fine qualities?"

Confucius said, "A gentleman is gracious without extravagance. He can work people without making them resentful. He has desires, but he is not greedy. He is composed, but not proud. He inspires awe, but he is not brutal."

Zi Zhang asked, "What do you mean by the first of these?"

Confucius said, "If he gives to the people only advantages they deserve, is he not being gracious without extravagance? If he imposes upon them only such tasks as they are capable of performing, is he not working them without making them resentful? If a man, out of desire for goodness, achieves it, how can he be greedy? A gentleman, irrespective of whether he is dealing with many persons or with few, with the small or with the great, never presumes to slight them, is not this indeed being composed without pride? A gentleman keeps his clothes and hat straight and his glances goodwilled and because of his seriousness, people feel a reverence as they look up at him——isn't this to inspire awe without brutality?"

Zi Zhang asked, "What are the four evils?"

Confucius said, "To put men to death without having taught them: This is cruelty. To expect the completion of tasks without giving proper advice: This is outrageousness. To insist upon punctual completion after instructions to proceed slowly: This is torment. To promise a reward but to begrudge its payment: This is pettiness."

子夏为莒父宰,问政。子曰:"无欲速,无见小利。欲速,则不达;见小利,则大事不成。"

(《论语·子路》)

〔译文〕子夏做了莒父县长,向孔子请教怎样管理政事。孔子说:"不要图快,不要贪求小利。图快而达不到目的;贪求小利就办不成大事。"

When Zi Xia became governor of Jufu County, he asked for advice about government. Confucius said, "Don't seek for haste, and don't concern yourself about little advantages. If you desire haste, you will not make real progress and achieve success. If you have an eye to little advantages, nothing important will ever get finished."

子曰:"能以礼让为国乎,何有? 不能以礼让为国,如礼何?"

(《论语·里仁》)

〔译文〕孔子说:"能够用礼让的原则来治理国家,那处理国事还有什么困难呢? 如果不能用礼让的原则来治理国家,那礼还有什么用呢?"

Confucius said, "Is it possible to govern a country by rites and yielding? There isn't any difficulty, is there? But if it is not really possible, of what use are rites?"

孟子曰:"城郭不完,兵甲不多,非国之灾也;田野不辟,货财不聚,非国之害也;上无礼,下无学,贼民兴,丧无日矣。"

(《孟子·离娄上》)

〔译文〕孟子说:"城墙不坚固,军备不充足,不是国家的灾难;田地没开辟,经济不宽裕,也不是国家的祸害;如果位于上面的人没有礼义,在下面的人没有教育,违法乱纪的人日益增多,国家的灭亡也就快了。"

Mencius said, "The country's disaster does not lie in that city walls aren't sturdy, soldiers and armours aren't sufficient, Nor does her scourge lie in that land isn't opened up and financial conditions aren't good. If the superiors don't implement rites and the inferiors receive no education, law and discipline breakers will be increasing and the country is soon to die out."

孔子曰:"……丘也闻有国有家者,不患寡而患不均,不患贫而患不安。盖均无贫,和无寡,安无倾。夫如是,故远人不服,则修文德以来之。既来之,则安之……"

(《论语·季氏》)

〔译文〕孔子说:"……我听说有国的诸侯、有家的大夫,不担心贫穷而担心财富不均,不担心人民稀少而担心不安定。财富均匀就不会有贫穷,彼此和睦人民自会不缺少,安定了便不会有倾复的危险。做到了这样,远方的人还不归服,就修仁义礼乐去招徕他们。他们已经来了,就让他们安心住下去……"

Confucius said, "I have heard that the head of a state or family must not worry about the santiness of wealth, but should worry about the unequal distribution of it, and that he must not worry about the small number of his people, but should worry about their unstability. For when wealth is equally distributed, there will be no poverty; when people are in harmony, there will be no lack of men; when there is stability throughout the land, there will be no danger of collapse. If all these are done, and yet the people of far-off lands still do not submit, then he should attract them by enhancing the prestige of his culture. Once they have been attracted, he should make them contented."

子曰:"不在其位,不谋其政。"

（《论语·泰伯》）

〔译文〕孔子说:"不在那个职位上,就不要考虑那方面的政事。"

Confucius said, "He who is not in charge of it does not interfere in its business."

子路问政。子曰:"先之劳之。"请益。曰:"无倦。"

（《论语·子路》）

〔译文〕子路问如何从政。孔子说:"让人家干的事你先干,然后才能让别人勤劳地工作。"子路请求多讲一些。孔子说:"办事不要懈怠。"

Zi Lu asked about governing. Confucius said, "Take the lead, then let others work hard." Zi Lu wanted additional advice. Confucius said, "Work untiringly."

子路问事君。子曰:"勿欺也,而犯之。"

(《论语·宪问》)

〔译文〕子路问怎样事奉君主,孔子说:"不要欺骗他,但可以规劝他。"

Zi Lu asked how to serve the monarch. Coufucius said, "Don't deceive him! But offer your exhortations if you have any objections."

孟子曰:"可以仕则仕,可以止则止,可以久则久,可以速则速。"

(《孟子·公孙丑上》)

〔译文〕孟子说:"应该做官就做官,应该辞职就辞职,应该继续干就继续干,应该马上走就马上走。"

Mencius said, "When you should secure an official position, secure it; when you should resign, resign; when you should go on to hold the post, hold it; when you should leave the post immediately, leave it immediately."

孟子曰:"君有过则谏,反复之而不听,则去。"

（《孟子·万章下》）

〔译文〕孟子说："君王有错误，要加以劝阻。如果反复劝阻还不听从，自己就要离职。"

Mencius said, "If the monarch has mistakes, we should talk him out of making mistakes. If we warn him again and again but he still does not listen, we should abandon the post."

孟子曰："夫人必自侮，然后人侮之；家必自毁，而后人毁之；国必自伐，而后人伐之。"

（《孟子·离娄上》）

〔译文〕孟子说："一个人有了自取侮辱的行为，别人才会侮辱他；一个家有了自取毁坏的因素，别人才能毁坏它；一个国家有了自取讨伐的原因，别人才讨伐它。"

Mencius said, "Only an individual's behaviour deserves insult, others could insult him. Only a home has the factors of being destroyed, others could destroy it. Only a country has the causes of being suppressed, others could send armed forces to suppress it."

孟子曰："夫物之不齐，物之情也；或相倍蓰，或相什百，或相千万。子比而同之,是乱天下也。巨屦小屦同贾,人岂为之哉? 从许子之道,相率而为伪者也,恶能治国家?"

(《孟子·滕文公上》)

〔译文〕孟子说:"各种东西不一样,是很自然的事。它们的价格有的相差一倍五倍,有的相差十倍百倍,也有的相差千倍万倍。你非要叫他们一样,只是扰乱天下罢了。不同质量的鞋一个价钱,人家肯干吗? 如果按照许行的学说办事,那就是引导大家不说实话,这又怎能治理好国家呢?"

Mencius said, "It's only natural that things are different. Some things are one to five times different in price. Some are ten or one hundred times and some are even one thousand or ten thousand times different. If You insist on that they should be the same, you are disturbing the world. Are people willing to sell both fine and bad shoes at the same price? If Master Xu's principles are followed it will lead people to utter false words. How can you run the country well this way?"

孟子曰:"易其田畴,薄其税敛,民可使富也。食之以时,用之以礼,财不可胜用也。"

(《孟子·尽心上》)

〔译文〕孟子说:"搞好耕种,减轻税收,可使百姓富足起来。按时食用,依照礼制消费,财物是用不尽的。"

Mencius said, "Good cultivation and less tax will make the common people rich. If they eat at proper times and consume in accordance with rites, property will never be used up."

孟子曰:"古之为市也,以其所有易其所无有,有司者治之耳。"

(《孟子·公孙丑下》)

[译文]孟子说:"古代的买卖,以有易无,这种事情,由相关的部门管理它。"

Mencius said, "In ancient time trade was done by exchanging what people had for what they did not have, This kind of business was managed by interrelated departments."

仁德篇第二

BOOK Ⅱ BENEVOLENCE

樊迟问仁。子曰:"爱人。"问知。子曰:"知人。"
樊迟未达。子曰:"举直错诸枉,能使枉者直。"

（《论语·颜渊》）

〔译文〕樊迟问什么是仁。孔子说:"爱人。"樊迟问什么是
智。孔子说:"善于鉴别人。"樊迟没有理解清楚。孔子说:"把
正直的人提拔起来,位置在邪恶人之上,就能使邪恶人变正
直。"

Fan Chi asked about benevolence, Confucius said, "To love
men." He asked about wisdom. Confucius said, "To know
men." Since Fan Chi did not quite understand, Confucius
continued, "If you will put upright persons above the crooked,
you will be making the crooked straight."

厩焚。子退朝,曰:"伤人乎?"不问马。

（《论语·乡党》）

〔译文〕马棚失火了。孔子退朝回来,说:"伤着人了吗?"
没有问马怎样。

When his stable was burnt down, on returning from the

court, Confucius said, "Was anyone hurt?" He did not ask about the horses.

子曰:"志士仁人,无求生以害人,有杀身以成仁。"

(《论语·卫灵公》)

[译文]孔子说:"一个有志气、品德高尚的人,从来不因贪生怕死而违背仁,只有勇于牺牲来成全仁。"

Confucius said, "Persons devoted to virtue and benevolenee will not seek to live at th expense of injuring benevolence, and will even sacrifice their lives to preserve it."

孟子曰:"仁,人心也;义,人路也。舍其路而弗由,放其心而不知求,哀哉! 人有鸡犬放,则知求之;有放心而不知求。学问之道无他,求其放心而已矣。"

(《孟子·告子上》)

[译文]孟子说:"仁是人的心;义是人的路。放弃正路不去走,丧失了良心不去求,实在太可悲了! 人丢了鸡犬,都知道去找;良心丢了却不知去找。治学问的道理没有别的,就是把丧失了的良心找回来就行了。"

Mencius said, "Benevolence is the human conscience;

justice is the road of life. What a great pity if one does not go on the correct road. What a great pity if one loses the conscience but does not seek it! If a person has lost his chicken or dog, he would go and find it. However, when he has lost his conscience, he does not know he should go and find it, The purpose of learning is nothing but trying to find one's lost conscience."

仲弓问仁。子曰:"出门如见大宾,使民如承大祭。己所不欲,勿施于人。在邦无怨,在家无怨。"

(《论语·颜渊》)

〔译文〕仲弓问什么是仁。孔子说:"当你出门做事时,就像接待贵宾一样认真,在你役使百姓时,就像承当重大祭祀一样谨慎。凡是自己不愿做的事情,不要强加到别人身上。在工作岗位上不对工作有怨气,在家里也没有怨气。"

Zhong Gong asked about benevolence. Confucius said, "When away from home, behave as though you would entertain a distinguished guest. Deal with the common people as though you were officiating at a solemn sacrifice. Do not do to others what you wouldn't like yourself. Do not have resentment in the affairs of the state or the family."

颜渊问仁。子曰:"克己复礼为仁。一日克己复礼,天下归仁焉。为仁由己,而由人乎哉?"

颜渊曰:"请问其目。"子曰:"非礼勿视,非礼勿听,非礼勿言,非礼勿动。"

(《论语·颜渊》)

〔译文〕颜渊问什么是仁。孔子说:"克制自己,使自己的言行合乎礼,这就是仁。一旦这样做了,天下人就会称许你是仁人。实行仁德,完全在于自己,难道在于别人吗?"颜渊说:"请问实行仁德的具体条件。"孔子说:"不合乎礼的东西不看,不合乎礼的话不听,不合乎礼的话不说,不合乎礼的事不做。"

Yan Yuan asked about benevolence. Confucius said, "He who can restrain himself and submit to rites is benevolent. Once he has succeeded in doing so, everyone under Heaven would honour him as a benevolent man. In putting benevolence into practice, one depends upon himself, not others."

Yan Yuan said, "I beg to ask for the guiding principles of conduct." Confucius said, "Look at nothing which is contrary to the rites; listen to nothing contrary to them; speak nothing contrary to them and do nothing contrary to them."

子张问仁于孔子。孔子曰:"能行五者于天下为仁矣。"

"请问之。"曰:"恭、宽、信、敏、惠。恭则不侮,宽则得众,信则人任焉,敏则有功,惠则足以使人。"

(《论语·阳货》)

〔译文〕子张问孔子怎样做才是仁。孔子说:"能够处处实行五种美德,就是仁人了。"子张说:"请问哪五种。"孔子说:"庄重,宽厚,诚实,勤敏,慈惠。庄重就不会招致侮辱,宽厚就能得到众人拥护,诚实就能得到别人的任用,勤敏就能取得成功,慈惠就会很好地使用人。"

Zi Zhang asked Confucius about benevolence. Confucius said, "He who could practise five things everywhere in the world would be benevolent." "What are they?" Zi Zhang asked. Confucius said, "Courtesy, magnanimity, sincerity, diligence and clemency. He who is courteous is not scorned, he who is magnanimous wins the multitude, he who is sincere is trusted by the people, he who is diligent succeeds in all he undertakes, he who is clement can get good service from the people."

樊迟问仁。子曰:"居处恭,执事敬,与人忠。虽之夷狄,不可弃也。"

(《论语·子路》)

〔译文〕樊迟问什么是仁。孔子说:"平时安居的时候,要端正恭谨,办起事来要严肃认真,与别人交往时要诚心诚意。即使到了落后的少数民族那里,也不能废弃这些做法。"

Fan Chi asked about benevolence. Confucius said, "In daily

life, upright and courteous; in business, earnest and diligent; in relationship, sincere and loyal. These precepts, even amid the barbarians, may not be set saide."

孟子曰:"分人之财谓之惠,教人以善谓之忠,为天下得人者谓之仁。"

(《孟子·滕文公上》)

[译文]孟子说:"把钱财分给别人叫做惠,把好的道理教给别人叫做忠,替天下找到出色的人才便叫做仁。"

Mencius said, "To distribute money or property among others is called kindness; to explain good principles to others is called honesty and to find people of talent and ability for the country is called benevolence."

子贡曰:"如有博施于民而能济众,何如? 可谓仁乎?"子曰:"何事于仁,必也圣乎! 尧舜其犹病诸! 夫仁者,己欲立而立人,己欲达而达人。能近取譬,可谓仁之方也已。"

(《论语·雍也》)

[译文]子贡说:"如果有人广泛地把好处给人民而且能够周济大众,这个人怎么样? 可以算得仁人吗?"孔子说:"何止是仁人,一定是圣人了! 尧舜恐怕都难以做到哩! 有仁德的

人,自己要站得住,也要使别人站得住;自己想事事行得通,也要使别人事事行得通。凡事能够推己及人,可以说是实行仁德的方法了。"

Zi Gong asked, "What would you say of a man if he not only conferred wide benefits upon the common people, but also compassed the salvation of all? Could such a man be called benevolent?" Confucius said, "It would no longer be a matter of benevolence. He would without doubt be a sage! Even Yao and Shun found it hard to succeed. I would describe benevolence like this: You yourself desire standing then help others to get standing. You yourself want success, then help others to attain success. Ability to draw analogies from oneself may be called the best way to implement benevolence."

子曰:"巧言令色,鲜矣仁!"

（《论语·学而》）

〔译文〕孔子说:"花言巧语,又装出一付伪善面孔,这种人,是很少仁德的啊!"

Confucius said, "Clever talk and a pretentious manner have little to do with benevolence."

孟子曰:"仁,人之安宅也;義,人之正路也。旷安宅而弗居,舍正路而不由,哀哉!"

(《孟子·离娄上》)

〔译文〕孟子说:"仁是人类安适的住宅;义是人类正确的道路。空着安适的住宅不去住,舍弃正确的道路不去走,是很可悲的啊!"

Mencius said, "Benevolence is the safe and comfortable dwelling place of human beings; righteousness is the right road for human beings to take. It is sad and miserable to leave the dwelling empty and abandon the road."

孟子曰:"仁之胜不仁也,犹水胜火。今之为仁者,犹以一杯水救一车薪之火也;不熄,则谓之水不胜火,此又与于不仁之甚者也,亦终必亡而已矣。"

(《孟子·告子上》)

〔译文〕孟子说;"仁能胜过不仁,正像水能灭火一样。如今行仁的人太少了,好像是用一杯水来扑灭一车柴木的火焰;火不灭,有人便说水不胜火,于是这些人又和不行仁的人同流合污,结果连自己的那一点点仁也丢掉了。"

Mencius said, "Benevolence will win non - benevolence, as water can put out fire. Nowadays, there are few people who implement benevolence, as a glass of water is used to put out fire caused by a cartful wood. The fire can't be put out, so someone says that water can not win fire. those who implement benevolence go along with those who do not in their evil deeds. As a result, the little benevolence they possess is lost, too."

子曰:"仁远乎哉? 我欲仁,斯仁至矣。"

(《论语·述而》)

〔译文〕孔子说:"仁难道离我们很远吗? 只要自己愿意实行仁,仁就可以来到。"

Confucius said, "Is benevolence indeed so far away? If we really want it, we will find it at our very side."

孟子曰:"五谷者,种之美者也;苟为不熟,不如荑稗。夫仁,亦在乎熟之而已矣。"

(《孟子·告子上》)

〔译文〕孟子说:"五谷是庄稼中的好品种;假若不成熟,还不如秭米和稗子。仁,也在于它真正能成熟罢了。"

Mencius said, "The five cereals(rice, two kinds of millet, wheat and beans)are the best species of all crops. If they are not ripe, however they are even worse than barnyard millet or grass. Real benevolence also lies in its maturity."

子曰:"知者不惑,仁者不忧,勇者不惧。"

(《论语·子罕》)

〔译文〕孔子说:"聪明的人不致疑惑,仁德的人经常乐观,勇敢的人无所畏惧。"

Confucius said, "He who is really wise can never be perplexed. He who is really of virtue and moralty can never be unhappy. He who is really brave is never fearful."

子曰:"有德者必有言,有言者不必有德。仁者必有勇,勇者不必有仁。"

(《论语·宪问》)

〔译文〕孔子说:"有道德的人一定有言论,但有言论的人不一定有道德。仁人一定勇敢,但勇敢的人不一定有仁德。"

Confucius said, "The man who has accumulated moral power will always have something to say, but those who do speak do not necessarily possess moral power. A benevolent man will certainly possess courage; but a brave man is not necessarily benevolent."

子曰:"知者乐水,仁者乐山。知者动,仁者静。知者乐,仁者寿。"

(《论语·雍也》)

〔译文〕孔子说:"聪明的人喜爱水,有仁德的人喜爱山。聪明的人活跃,有仁德的人安静。聪明的人生活快乐,有仁德的人则长寿。"

Confucius said, "The wise delight in water, the virtuous delight in mountains. The wise are active, the virtuous stay still. The wise are happy, the virtuous are long-lived."

子曰:"当仁,不让于师。"

(《论语·卫灵公》)

〔译文〕孔子说:"面对关于仁德的事情,可以不必对老师谦让。"

Confucius said, "When it comes to benevolence, one need not avoid competing with his teacher."

孟子曰:"人之所以异于禽兽者几希,庶民去之,君子存之。舜明于庶物,察于人伦,由仁义行,非行仁义也。"

(《孟子·离娄下》)

〔译文〕孟子说:"人和禽兽不同的地方廖廖无几,普通百姓丢了它,有道德的君子却保存了它。舜懂得事物的道理,了解人们之间的关系,所以他从仁义之路而行,而不是把仁义仅仅当作工具或手段来使用。"

Mencius said,"Human beings are different from birds and beasts only in several aspects. Common people have lost them, but the virtuous gentlemen have retained them. Shun knew the principles of things and understood the relationships among people. He took the road of benevolence and righteousness, and he did not take them as a tool or means."

子曰:"富与贵,是人之所欲也;不以其道得之,不处也。贫与贱,是人之所恶也;不以其道得之,不去也。君子去仁,恶乎成名? 君子无终食之间违仁,造次必于是,颠沛必于是。"

(《论语·里仁》)

〔译文〕孔子说:"金钱和地位,这是人人所想望的;不是通过正当的方法得到它,君子不享受。贫穷和下贱,这是人人所厌恶的;不是通过正当的方法摆脱它们,君子不去摆脱。君子离开了仁德,怎么能成名呢? 君子应该连吃饭这么短的时间也不违背仁,在匆忙急切的时候要保持仁德,颠沛流离的时候同样也要保持仁德。"

Confucius said, "Wealth and rank are what everyone desires; but if they can only be obtained by improper way, a gentleman must not accept them. Poverty and meanness are what everyone abhors; but if they are to be removed by improper way, he can not release from them. If a gentleman ever parts with benevolence, how can he achieve his fame? Never for a moment does a gentleman go against benevolence. He is with benevolence all the time, even when he hurries and wanders about in a desperate flight."

子曰:"里仁为美。择不处仁,焉得知?"

(《论语·里仁》)

[译文]孔子说:"住的地方,要有仁德才好。选择住处,不居住在有仁德的地方,怎么能说是聪明呢?"

Confucius said, "To live among the benevolent is the finest thing possible. How can a man be considered wise if, when he has the choice, he does not prefer to live in such surroundings?"

子曰:"人而不仁,如礼何? 人而不仁,如乐何?"

（《论语·八佾》）

〔译文〕孔子说："一个人没有仁爱之心，还能讲礼吗？一个人没有仁爱之心，还能讲音乐吗？"

Confucius said, "A man without charity in his heart - what has he to do with rites? A man without charity in his heart - what has he to do with music?"

子曰："人之过也，各于其党。观过，斯知仁矣。"

（《论语·里仁》）

〔译文〕孔子说："人们所犯的错误，都和他们为人的类别有关。考察所犯错误的性质，就可以知道他们的仁德水平了。"

Confucius said, "Men's faults are always related to the types of their personality. By examing the different nature of their faults, we can tell how they are adherent to benevolence."

子贡问为仁。子曰："工欲善其事，必先利其器。居是邦也，事其大夫之贤者，友其士之仁者。"

（《论语·卫灵公》）

〔译文〕子贡问怎样培养仁德。孔子说:"工匠要搞好工作,一定要准备好工具。我们住在一个国家内,就要敬奉那些大官中的贤人,结交那些士人中的仁人。"

Zi Gong asked how to become good. Confucius said, "A craftsman, if he means to do good work, must first sharpen his tools. In whatever state you live, what is most important is to honour the virtuous among the senior officials, and to associate with the humane among the gentry."

子曰:"泰伯,其可谓至德也已矣。三以天下让,民无得而称焉。"

(《论语》·泰伯)

〔译文〕孔子说:"泰伯,可以说是品德最高尚了。他多次把君位让给弟弟季历,老百姓简直找不出恰当的词语来称赞他。"

Confucius said, "Tai Bo can certainly be called a man of virtue and morality. No less than three times he renounced the throne in favour of his younger brother. The common people couldn't find proper words to praise him for it."

子曰:"巍巍乎,舜、禹之有天下也,而不与焉。"

（《论语》·泰伯）

〔译文〕孔子说："舜和禹真是崇高得很呀！他们虽拥有天下,却一点也不为自己。"

Confucius said, "Noble were Shun and Yu! All that is under Heaven was theirs, yet they remained aloof from it."

孟子曰："鱼,我所欲也,熊掌亦我所欲也;二者不可得兼,舍鱼而取熊掌者也。生亦我所欲也,义亦我所欲也;二者不可得兼,舍生而取义者也。"

（《孟子·告子上》)

〔译文〕孟子说："我喜欢鱼,我也喜欢熊掌;如果两样不能并有,我便丢掉鱼而要熊掌。我喜爱生命,我也喜爱义;如果两样不能并有,我便舍弃生命而要义。"

Mencius said, "Fish is what I want to have, a bear's paw is what I want to have. If I can take only one of the two, I would prefer a bear's paw to fish, Life is what I treasure, righteousness is what I treasure. If I can possess only one of the two, I would prefer righteousness to life."

孟子曰："尊德乐义,则可以嚣嚣矣。故士穷不失义,达不离道。穷不失义,故士得己焉;达不离道,故民不失望焉。古之人,得志,泽加于民;不得志,修身见于世。穷则独善其身,达则兼善天下。"

(《孟子·尽心上》)

〔译文〕孟子说:"崇尚德,喜爱义,就可以自得其乐了。所以,士人穷困时不要丢掉义,顺利时不要离开道。穷困时不失掉义,才能自得其乐;顺利时不离开道,百姓才不致失望。古人得志时,给百姓一些好处;不得志时,修养自己的品德并以此表现于世人。穷困时把自身修养完善,顺利时为天下多做些好事。"

Mencius said, "If one cherishes virtue and loves righteousness, he will be content with his lot. So a bachelor shouldn't give up righteousness when he is in poverty, nor principles when he is successful. Only when a bachelor retains righteousness in poverty, can he be content with his lot. Also, only when he does not deviate from principle while successful do common people not feel disappointed. When the ancients achieved their ambitions, they bestowed kindness and favours on the common people. But when they suffered from setbacks, they cultivated their virtue and showed it to the society. They paid attention to their own moral uplift when in poverty and did more good things for the country when successful."

孟子曰:"杀一无罪非仁也;非其有而取之非义也。居恶在? 仁是也。路恶在? 义是也。居仁由义,大人之事备矣。"

(《孟子·尽心上》)

[译文]孟子说:"杀一个无罪的人,是不仁;不应为自己所有,却去拿来,是不义。所住的地方在那里呢? 仁便是。所行的道路在那里呢? 义便是。居住于仁,行走于义,一个有身份的人的工作便算齐备了。"

Mencius said, "One is unbenevolent if he kills one innocent person. One is unrighteous if he takes anything that does not belong to him. Where is the place to live in? It is where there is benevolence. Where is the road to go on? It is where there is righteousness. The working conditions are ready for a person of rank and position if he lives in benevolence and walks about on righteousness."

孟子曰:"恻隐之心,人皆有之;羞恶之心,人皆有之;恭敬之心,人皆有之;是非之心,人皆有之。恻隐之心,仁也;羞恶之心,义也;恭敬之心,礼也;是非之心,智也。仁义礼智,非由外铄我也,我固有之也,弗思耳矣。"

(《孟子·告子上》)

[译文]孟子说:"同情心,人人都有;羞耻心,人人都有;恭敬心,人人都有;是非心,人人都有。同情心属于仁;羞恶心属

于义;恭敬心属于礼;是非心属于智。这仁义礼智,不是外人给与我的,是我本来就有的,只是没有去探索追求罢了。"

Mencius said, "Everyone has sympathy, sense of shame, sense of respectfulness, and sense of right and wrong, Sympathy belongs to benevolence; the sense of shame belongs to justice; the sense of respectfulness belongs to rites; the sense of right and wrong belongs to wisdom. Benevolence, justice, rites and wisdom are not forced to me by others; they are inherent in me. Nevertheless, I haven't reflected on them yet."

修养篇第三

BOOK Ⅲ
SELF – CULTIVATION

子谓子产，"有君子之道四焉：其行己也恭，其事上也敬，其养民也惠，其使民也义。"

（《论语·公冶长》）

[译文]孔子评论子产，说："他具有君子的四种道德：他自己的行为庄重，他事奉君主恭敬，他抚育人民有恩惠，他役使人民合乎道理。"

Of Zi Chan Confucius said, "In him were to be found four of the virtues that belong to true gentlemen. In his private conduct he was courteous; in serving his master, he was respectful; in providing for the needs of the people he was gracious; in exacting service from the people, he was just and reasonable."

子曰："质胜文则野，文胜质则史。文质彬彬，然后君子。"

（《论语·雍也》）

[译文]孔子说："一个人质朴超过文采，那就未免粗野；如果文采胜过质朴，又未免浮夸。如果文采和质朴在一个人身上班班相称，这才叫做君子。"

Confucius said, "When honesty overbalances refinement, crudeness results. When refinement overbalances honesty, there is superficiality. Only when refinement and honesty are duly balanced will gentlemen emerge."

子曰:"君子义以为质,礼以行之,孙以出之,信以成之。君子哉!"

(《论语·卫灵公》)

〔译文〕孔子说:"君子以义作为做人的根本,用礼仪来实行它,用谦逊的语言来说出它,用诚实的态度去完成它。这才是君子啊!"

Confucius said, "A gentleman takes justice as men's essence and he takes rites as the guide in putting it into practice. He is modest in saying it and faithful in accomplishing it. That man is indeed a true gentleman."

孟子曰:"君子所以异於人者,以其存心也。君子以仁存心,以礼存心。仁者爱人,有礼者敬人。"

(《孟子·离娄下》)

〔译文〕孟子说:"君子同普通人的差别,在于居心不同。君子居心于仁和礼。仁人爱别人,有礼的人恭敬别人。"

Mencius said, "The difference between a gentleman and the common people lies in what they care about. A gentleman cares about benevolence and ritual. The benevolent love others and the ritual respect others."

子贡问君子。子曰:"先行其言而后从之。"

(《论语·为政》)

〔译文〕子贡问怎样才能做一名君子。孔子说:"君子总是把想要说的话先实行了,再说出来。"

Zi Gong asked how to be a gentleman. Confucius said, "A gentleman does not preach what he practises till he has practised what he preaches."

孟子曰:"亲亲而仁民,仁民而爱物。"

(《孟子·尽心上》)

〔译文〕孟子说:"君子亲爱自己的亲人,因而对百姓仁爱。因为对百姓仁爱,所以便爱惜万物。"

Mencius said, "Since a gentleman is dear to his family members, he is benevolent to the common people. And since he

is benevolent to the common people, he treasures everything in
the world."

孟子曰："富贵不能淫,贫贱不能移,威武不能屈。此之谓
大丈夫。"

(《孟子·滕文公下》)

〔译文〕孟子说:"富贵不能扰乱他的心,贫贱不能改变他
的志向,威武不能屈辱他的气节。这样才叫作大丈夫。"

Mencius said, "Neither wealth nor honours can lead him
astray; neither poverty nor destitution can change his ideal and
he is not to be subdued by force. This kind of man can be called
a real man."

子曰:"君子有九思:视思明,听思聪,色思温,貌思恭,言
思忠,事思敬,疑思问,忿思难,见得思义。"

(《论语·季氏》)

〔译文〕孔子说:"君子要用心思考九件事:看的时候要考
虑是否看明白了,听的时候要考虑是否听清楚了,脸的颜色要
考虑是否温和,容貌态度要考虑是否恭敬,说话交谈要考虑是
否忠诚,对待工作要考虑是否认真,遇到疑问要考虑怎样向人
家请教,发怒的时候要考虑是否有后患,看见可得的要考虑是

否合乎义。"

Confucius said, "There are nine things of which a gentleman must be mindful: to see clearly when he looks, to hear distinctively when he listens, to be gentle in his looks, to be respectful in his manners, to be faithful in words, to be earnest in service, to enquire politely when in doubt, to think of consequences in anger, to think of justice when he sees an advantage."

孔子曰："君子有三戒：少之时，血气未定，戒之在色；及其壮也，血气方刚，戒之在斗；及其老也，血气既衰，戒之在得。"
（《论语·季氏》）

〔译文〕孔子说："君子要警惕三件事：年少时，血气没有稳定，要警惕不要贪恋女色；到了壮年，血气正当旺盛，要警惕不要争强好斗；到了老年，血气已经衰退，要警惕不要贪得无厌。"

Confucius said, "There are three things against which a gentleman should be on his guard. In youth, before his pulse has settled down, he is on his guard against lust. Having reached his prime, when his pulse has become strong, he is on his guard against strife. Having reached old age, when his pulse declines, he is on his guard against avarice."

孟子曰:"君子有三乐,而王天下不与存焉。父母俱存,兄弟无故,一乐也;仰不愧于天,俯不怍于人,二乐也;得天下英才而教之,三乐也。君子有三乐,而王天下不与存焉。"

(《孟子·尽心上》)

〔译文〕孟子说:"君子有三种乐趣,但是以德服天下并不在其中。父母都健在,兄弟没灾患,是第一种乐趣;抬头对得起天,低头对得起人,是第二种乐趣;得到天下优秀的人才而对他们进行教育,是第三种乐趣。君子有三种乐趣,但是以德服天下并不在其中。"

Mencius said, "The gentleman has three kinds of joys, The first joy is that his parents are still in good health and his brothers suffer no calamities. The second joy is that he has not let God down on the one hand, and on the other, he has treated people fairly. The third joy is that he can have the outstanding people of the world to teach. The virtuous person has three kinds of joys, but convincing the world by virtues is not among these."

孟子曰:"君子居是国也,其君用之,则安富尊荣;其子弟从之,则孝悌忠信。"

(《孟子·尽心上》)

〔译文〕孟子说:"君子居住在一个国家里,君王如果使用他,就会平安、富足、尊贵而有名誉;少年子弟如果跟从他,就会孝敬父母,敬爱兄长,忠心而守信实。"

Mencius said, "A gentleman lives in a country. When the monarch uses him, he will enjoy safety, prosperity, respect and honour; when young people follow him, they will be filial, respectful, loyal and honest."

子曰:"君子无所争。必也射乎! 揖让而升,下而饮。其争也君子。"

(《论语·八佾》)

〔译文〕孔子说:"君子没有什么可争的事情。如果有所争,一定是比箭吧! 即使是比箭,也是先互相作揖、谦让,然后上场。射箭完毕走下场来,又互相敬酒。这样仍不失为君子。"

Confucius said, "Gentlemen never compete. If, they do it in archery. But even then they bow and make way for each other when they are going up to the archery – ground. After the competition they come down and drink together. Thus, even when competing they remain gentlemen."

孟子曰:"体有贵贱,有小大。无以小害大,无以贱害贵。养其小者为小人,养其大者为大人。"

(《孟子·告子上》)

〔译文〕孟子说:"人的身体有重要部分和不重要的部分,有大处,也有小处。不要因保养小的部位而影响大的部位,不要因为保护次要的部分而影响了重要的部分。只保养小部位的人是小人,而保养身体中大部位的人则是君子。"

Mencius said,"The human body has its important parts and unimportant parts, as well as big parts and small parts. One should not endanger the big parts when taking care of the small parts, nor do harm to the important parts when protecting the unimportant parts. Those who only take good care of the small parts are base persons, While those who take good care of the big parts are gentlemen."

子曰:"君子之于天下也,无适也,无莫也,义之与比。"

(《论语·里仁》)

〔译文〕孔子说:"君子处理天下的事情,没有一定要怎样做,也没有一定不要怎样做,而是怎样做合理恰当,就怎样做。"

Confucius said, "A gentleman in his dealings with the world shows no preferences, but he is prejudiced in favour of what is right."

孟子曰:"君子深造之以道,欲其自得之也。自得之,则居之安;居之安,则资之深;资之深,则取之左右逢其原。故君子欲其自得之也。"

(《孟子·离娄下》)

〔译文〕孟子说:"君子按照正确的方法来得到高深的造诣,就是要他自觉地有所得。自觉地有所得,就能牢固掌握此方法而不动摇;牢固地掌握它而不动摇,就能将德行积蓄很深;积蓄很深,就能任意择取,左右逢源。因此君子在培养自己的道德时就应该自觉地有所得。"

Mencius said, "When a gentleman wants to achieve great attainments according to the correct method, he should do this conscientiously. In this way, he can have sound mastery of the method. The sound mastery will let him have many qualifications. When he has many qualifications, he can make free choices and achieve success one way or another. So a gentleman should achieve conscientiously when he is cultivating his virtues."

孟子去齐,充虞路问曰:"夫子若有不豫色然。前日虞闻诸夫子曰:'君子不怨天,不尤人。'"

(《孟子·公孙丑下》)

〔译文〕孟子离开齐国,充虞在路上对他说:"您看起来似乎不高兴。但我从前听您说过:'君子不抱怨天,也不责怪别人。'"

Mencius left the Qi state. On the way Chong Yu said to him, "You look unhappy, but I once heard you say, 'A gentleman never complain about the Heaven, nor does he blame others.'"

孟子曰:"夫义,路也;礼,门也。惟君子能由是路,出入是门也。"

(《孟子·万章下》)

〔译文〕孟子说:"义好比是大路;礼好比是大门。只有君子能从这大路上行走,由这处大门出进。"

Mencius said, "Righteousness is just like a road; ritual is just like a gate. Only a gentleman can walk on the road, come and go through the gate."

子曰："君子矜而不争,群而不党。"

(《论语·卫灵公》)

〔译文〕孔子说:"君子态度庄重而不与人争执,能够合群而不与人勾结。"

Confucius said, "A gentleman is dignified but not quarrelsome;sociable,but not clannish."

子曰："君子不以言举人,不以人废言。"

(《论语·卫灵公》)

〔译文〕孔子说:"君子不以某人说得话好听而抬举他,也不以某人品德不好而废弃他说的正确话。"

Confucius said, "A gentleman does not accept a man for his words alone, nor does he reject a good suggestion because of the man alone."

子曰："君子欲讷于言而敏于行。"

(《论语·里仁》)

〔译文〕孔子说:"君子应该说话谨慎而行动敏捷。"

Confucius said,"A gentleman should be cautious in word, but prompt in deed."

孟子曰:"君子不亮,恶乎执?"

（《孟子·告子下》）

〔译文〕孟子说:"君子如果不讲诚信,如何能有操守?"

Mencius said,"If a gentleman is not upright,how could he has personal integrity?"

子曰:"君子病无能焉,不病人之不己知也。"

（《论语·卫灵公》）

〔译文〕孔子说:"君子忧虑自己没有才能,而不忧虑别人不了解自己。"

Confucius said,"A gentleman is distressed by his own lack of capacity;he is never distressed at others' failure to recognize his merits."

子曰:"君子耻其言而过其行。"

（《论语·宪问》）

〔译文〕孔子说:"说得多,做得少,君子以为可耻。"

Confucius said, "A gentleman is ashamed to let his words outrun his deeds."

子曰:"古者言之不出,耻躬之不逮也。"

(《论语·里仁》)

〔译文〕孔子说:"古人不轻易把话说出口,因为他们以说得出而做不到为耻辱。"

Confucius said, "The ancients kept a hold on their words, fearing the disgrace that would ensue if they failed to keep pace with them."

孟子曰:"志士不忘在沟壑,勇士不忘丧其元。"

(《孟子·滕文公下》)

〔译文〕孟子说:"有志气的人不怕死后弃尸山沟,勇敢的人不怕丢了脑袋。"

Mencius said, "A strong－willed man is not afraid of his body being thrown into a gully after his death. A brave man is not afraid of losing his head."

　　孟子曰:"且古之君子,过则改之;今之君子,过则顺之。古之君子,其过也,如日月之食,民皆见之;及其更也,民皆仰之。今之君子,岂徒顺之,又从为之辞。"

　　　　　　　　　　　　　　　　(《孟子·公孙丑下》)

　　〔译文〕孟子说:"古代的君子,有了过错,随即改正;今天的君子,有了过错,竟将错就错。古代君子的过错,好像日蚀、月蚀,百姓都能看得到;当他改正的时候,人们都抬头望着。今天的君子,不仅将错就错,并且还编造出一套假道理来为自己的错误辩护。"

Mencius said, "When the ancient gentleman made a mistake, he would correct it immediately. In contrast, when the current gentleman makes a mistake, he leaves it uncorrected and even makes the best of it. The ancient gentleman's mistake was like the solar eclipse or the lunar eclipse; the common people all saw it very clearly. When he was correcting his mistake, all people raised their heads to see it. The current gentleman not only leaves his mistake uncorrected and makes the best of it, but also fabricates a set of false reasons to defend himself."

　　子曰:"君子周而不比,小人比而不周。"

（《论语·为政》）

〔译文〕孔子说："君子讲团结而不互相勾结，小人互相勾结而不讲团结。"

Confucius said,"A gentleman stresses unity, but he is free from collusion. The petty man acts reversely."

子曰："君子和而不同，小人同而不和。"

（《论语·子路》）

〔译文〕孔子说："君子讲协调而不盲目附和，小人盲目附和而不讲协调。"

Confucius said,"The true gentleman is conciliatory but not blind – accommodating. Petty men are blind – accommodating but not conciliatory."

子曰："君子求诸己，小人求诸人。"

（《论语·卫灵公》）

〔译文〕孔子说："君子严格要求自己，小人苛刻要求别人。"

Confucius said, "A gentleman makes demands of himself; the petty man, of others."

子曰:"君子喻于义,小人喻于利。"
　　　　　　　　　　　　　　(《论语·里仁》)

[译文]孔子说:"君子懂得大义,小人懂得的是小利。"

Confucius said, "A gentleman is conscious only of justice, a petty man, only of self‑interest."

子曰:"君子上达,小人下达。"
　　　　　　　　　　　　　　(《论语·宪问》)

[译文]孔子说:"君子通达于仁义,小人通达于财利。"

Confucius said, "The gentleman reaches complete understanding of what is just and benevolent; the petty man reaches complete understanding of what is profitable."

子曰:"君子坦荡荡,小人长戚戚。"
　　　　　　　　　　　　　　(《论语·述而》)

〔译文〕孔子说："君子胸怀宽广,小人经常忧愁。"

Confucius said, "A true gentleman is calm and at ease; a petty man is always worried and full of distress."

子曰："君子泰而不骄,小人骄而不泰。"
（《论语·子路》）

〔译文〕孔子说："君子安详舒泰而不骄傲凌人,小人骄傲凌人却不安详舒泰。"

Confucius said, "The gentleman is dignified, but never haughty; the petty man is haughty, but never dignified."

子曰："君子成人之美,不成人之恶。小人反是。"
（《论语·颜渊》）

〔译文〕孔子说："君子总爱成全人家的好事,不去促成人家的坏事。小人却与此相反。"

Confucius said, "A gentleman enables the good wishes of others, not their bad ones. A petty man does just the reverse of this."

子欲居九夷。或曰:"陋,如之何?"子曰:"君子居之,何陋
之有?"

(《论语·子罕》)

〔译文〕孔子想到九夷去居住。有人说:"那地方非常简
陋,怎么好住?"孔子说:"有君子住到那里去,就不简陋了。"

Confucius wanted to settle among the Nine Wild Tribes
(of the East). Someone said, "I am afraid you would find it
hard to put up with their lack of refinement."Confucius said,
"Were a true gentleman to settle among them, then there would
soon be no problem about the lack of refinement." (His
presence would alter all that.)

子曰:"吾十有五而志于学,三十而立,四十而不惑,五十
而知天命,六十而耳顺,七十而从心所欲,不逾矩。"

(《论语·为政》)

〔译文〕孔子说:"我从十五岁立志学习,三十岁便能在社
会上立身处世做人,四十岁便懂得各种知识而不致迷惑,五十
岁可以知道天地间事物的运行规律,六十岁听到别人说话就
能辨明是非真假,七十岁心里怎样想便能怎样做,而不会超越
规矩。"

Confucius said, "At fifteen I set my heart upon learning. At thirty I was firmly established. At forty I had no more doubts. At fifty I knew the rules of things in the universe. At sixty I could judge correctly whatever I had heard. At seventy I could follow my heart's desire without violating the regulations."

子曰:"见贤思齐焉,见不贤而内自省也。"

(《论语·里仁》)

〔译文〕孔子说:"看见贤人,就应该想向他看齐。看见不贤的人,就应该反省自己有什么不贤的地方。"

Confucius said, "When you see a good man, think of emulating him; when you see a bad man, examine yourself."

孔子曰:"见善如不及,见不善如探汤。吾见其人矣,吾闻其语矣……。"

(《论语·季氏》)

〔译文〕孔子说:"看见好的言行,就像怕赶不上一样地努力追求;看见不好的言行,就像把手伸到开水里一样赶快避开。我看见过这样的人,我也听到过这样的话。

Confucius said, "When seeing what is good, pursue it as though you could never quite come to it; when seeing what is not good, elude it as though you dared not put your fingers into boiling water. I have heard this saying and I have seen such men.

曹交问曰:"人皆可以为尧舜,有诸?"
孟子曰:"然。"

(《孟子·告子下》)

〔译文〕曹交问道:"人人都可以成为尧舜这样的人,有这种说法吗?"
孟子说:"有的。"

Tsao Jiao asked, "Is there such a saying that everyone can be a good person like Emperor Yao or Emperor Shun?"
Mencius said, "Yes, there is."

樊迟从游于舞雩之下,曰:"敢问崇德、修慝、辨惑。"子曰:"善哉问! 先事后得,非崇德与? 攻其恶,无攻人之恶,非修慝与? 一朝之忿,忘其身,以及其身,非惑与?"

(《论语·颜渊》)

〔译文〕樊迟跟着孔子在舞雩台下游玩,说:"请问怎样提高自己的品德,改正过失、辨别是非。"孔子说:"问得好!工作在先,享受在后,不是提高品德了吗? 检讨自己的错误,不指责别人的错误,这不是改正了过失吗? 由于一时的气愤,便忘掉了自身的安危,以至牵连到自己的亲人,这不是糊涂吗?"

Once when Fan Chi was taking a walk with Confucius at the site of the Rain Dance Altars, he asked about how to enhance one's virtue, correct one's mistakes, and tell the true from the false. Confucius said, "What good questions! Consider your job of prime importance; put the reward in second place——isn't that enhancing virtue? Attack the evil that is within yourself; do not attack the evil that is in others——isn't that correcting mistakes? In a moment's burst of anger to forget one's own safety and even endanger one's family—— isn't that utter confusion?"

孟子曰:"故天将降大任于是人也。必先苦其心志,劳其筋骨,饿其体肤,空乏其身,行拂乱其所为,所以动心忍性,曾益其所不能。"

(《孟子·告子下》)

〔译文〕孟子说:"所以天将要把重大的任务加到某人身上,必须先苦恼他的心志,劳动他的筋骨,饥饿他的肠胃,穷困他的身子,使他的每一种行为都不能如意,从而可以震动他的心意,坚韧他的性情,增强他的能力。"

Mencius said, "So, if God would give an important task to a certain person, the first things He does are to temper his willpower, fatigue his muscles and bones, starve his stomach and destitute his body. God would not make any kind of his action satisfactory as he wishes in order to shock his heart, make his temperament persistent and dauntless, and increase his ability."

孟子曰:"老吾老,以及人之老;幼吾幼,以及人之幼。天下可运于掌。"

(《孟子·梁惠王上》)

〔译文〕孟子说:"尊敬自己的长辈,从而推广到尊敬别人的长辈;爱护自己的晚辈,从而推广到爱护别人的晚辈。那么,要统一天下就好像一件东西在手中运转那么容易了。"

Mencius said, "Show respect to one's seniors and further to others; take care of one's juniors and then of others. Then it is as easy to unify the country as turn something round in the hand."

孟子曰:"养心莫善于寡欲。其为人也寡欲,虽有不存焉者,寡矣;其为人也多欲,虽有存焉者,寡矣。"

（《孟子·尽心下》）

[译文]孟子说:"修养心性最好的办法是减少物质欲望。一个人如果欲望不多,他的善性虽然有所丧失,但不会多;一个人如果欲望太多,他的善性虽然有所保存,也是极少的了。"

Mencius said, "The best way to cultivate one's nature is to reduce one's material desires. If a person does not have many desires, even he loses a little of his good nature, he would not lose much. If a person has many material desires, even his good nature is kept to some extent, it would be very little."

孟子曰:"爱人者,人恒爱之;敬人者,人恒敬之。"

（《孟子·离娄下》）

[译文]孟子说:"爱别人的人,会经常受到别人的爱;尊敬别人的人,会经常受到别人尊敬。"

Mencius said, "Those who love others would be loved by others. Those who respect others would be respected by others."

子曰:"不患人之不己知,患其不能也。"

（《论语·宪问》）

〔译文〕孔子说:"不要担心别人不了解自己,担心的是自己没有才能。"

Confucius said, "Be not concerned over men's not knowing of you; be concerned rather over your own incapacities."

孟子曰:"爱人不亲,反其仁;治人不治,反其智;礼人不答,反其敬——行有不得者皆反求诸己,其身正而天下归之。"

(《孟子·离娄上》)

〔译文〕孟子说:"我爱别人,但别人并不亲近我,那就要反过头来看看自己的仁爱够不够;我管别人,可是管不好,那就要反过头来看看自己的智慧够不够;我以礼待人,大家不理我,那就要反过头来看看自己是否真的恭敬——任何行为如果得不到预期的效果,均应反过头来检查自己,自己的行为端正了,天下人自会归附自己。"

Mencius said, "When I love others but others are not on intimate terms with me, I would examine myself to see whether my kindheartedness has been enough. When I supervise others but I can not do it well, I would examine myself to see whether I have the ability. When I treat others with due respect but others ignore me, I would examine myself to see whether I am really respectful to others. In short, if any behaviour does not produce corresponding effect, one should examine oneself. Only one's behaviour being correct, can one enjoy the inclination of the hearts of all people."

子曰:"德不孤,必有邻。"

(《论语·里仁》)

[译文]孔子说:"有道德的人是不会孤单的,必定会有志同道合的人与之相伴。"

Confucius said, "A man of morality will never live in solitude; he will always bring companions."

孟子曰:"吾未闻枉己而正人者也,况辱己以正天下者乎? 圣人之行不同也,或远,或近,或去,或不去;归洁其身而已矣。"

(《孟子·万章上》)

[译文]孟子说:"我没有听说过自己不正直,却能叫别人正直的,何况那种先使自己受辱,再去匡正天下的做法呢? 圣人的行为各不相同,他们对当时的君主有的疏远,有的靠拢,有的离开,有的不离开;但归根结底,都使自己干干净净,不沾上肮脏东西。"

Mencius said, "I have never heard the saying that one is not just oneself but can make others to be just, let alone the practice that one is disgraced oneself but wants to correct the world. The sage's behaviours are not like that. They took different attitudes towards their contemporary monarchs: from some monarch they would become estranged, to some, they would be closer, some they would leave, and some they would not leave; eventually, they would make themselves clean and not be tainted with dirt."

佛肸召,子欲往。子路曰:"昔者由也闻诸夫子曰:'亲于其身为不善者,君子不入也'。佛肸以中牟畔,子之往也,如之何?"

子曰:"然,有是言也。不曰坚乎,磨而不磷;不曰白乎,涅而不缁。吾岂匏瓜也哉? 焉能系而不食?"

(《论语·阳货》)

〔译文〕佛肸召孔子,孔子想去。子路说:"过去我听老师说过:'亲身做坏事的人那里,君子是不去的。'佛肸以中牟为据点反叛,您却要去,怎么能这样做呢?"孔子说:"是的,我是说过这样的话。但是,不是也说过坚硬的东西,磨也磨不薄吗? 不是说过洁白的东西,染也染不黑吗? 我难道是只苦葫芦,只能系挂着而不给人吃吗?"

When Bi Xi of the Jin State sommoned Confucius, he

wanted to go. Then Zi Lu said, "I remember you once saying, 'A gentleman will never enter the house of one who is in his own person doing what is evil.' Now Bi Xi is holding Zhongmu in revolt. How can you think of going to him?" Confucius said, "It is true that there is such a thing. But isn't it also said that there are things so hard that no grinding will ever wear them down, that there are things so white that no dyeing will ever make them black? Am I indeed to be forever like the bitter gourd that is only fit to hang up, but not to eat?"

子曰:"富而可求也,虽执鞭之士,吾亦为之。如不可求,从吾所好。"

(《论语·述而》)

〔译文〕孔子说:"财富如果可以合理地求得,即使是替人执鞭的下等差役,我也愿意去做。如果财富不能合理地求得,那我还是干我所爱好的事情。"

Confucius said, "I would adopt any means of obtaining wealth without doing wrong, even if it means being a carrige driver. But so long as it is a question of illegitimate means, I shall continue to pursue the quests that I love."

孟子曰:"言近而指远者,善言也;守约而施博者,善道也。

君子之言也,不下带而道存焉;君子之守,修其身而天下平。人病舍其田而芸人之田——所求于人者重,而所以自任者轻。"

(《孟子·尽心下》)

〔译文〕孟子说:"言语浅近而意义深远的,叫做善言;所办的事简单而效果很大的,叫做善道。君子的言语,讲的虽是常见的事情,里面却蕴藏着道;君子的操守,从修养自己开始然后影响到别人,从而使天下太平。一个人的毛病在于放弃自己的田地,却去种别人的田地——也就是说要求别人多而严,自己负担的任务却是少而宽。"

Mencius said, "Words that are easy to understand but have profound and lasting meanings are called good words; Deeds that are simple but very influential are called good deeds. A gentleman's words refer to common things but imply principles. A gentleman's principle of personal integrity is that he cultivates himself first, then influences others until there is peace all over the world. A person's defect lies in abandoning his own land but cultivating that of others, that is, asking others to do much but shouldering little and light work himself."

子曰:"贫而无怨难,富而无骄易。"

(《论语·宪问》)

〔译文〕孔子说:"贫穷而没有怨言很难,富有而不骄傲倒容易做到。"

Confucius said, "To be poor and not resent it is far harder than to be rich, yet not presumptuous."

子曰:"饭疏食饮水,曲肱而枕之,乐亦在其中矣。不义而富且贵,于我如浮云。"

(《论语·述而》)

〔译文〕孔子说:"吃粗粮,喝冷水,弯着胳膊当枕头,这里面自有乐趣。用不正当的手段得来的富贵,在我看来好像浮云一样。"

Confucius said, "With coarse food to eat, cold water to drink, and the bended arm as a pillow, happiness may still exsist. Wealth and rank unrighteously obtained seem to me as insubstantial as floating clouds."

孟子曰:"欲贵者,人之同心也。人人有贵于己者,弗思耳矣。人之所贵者,非良贵也。"

(《孟子·告子上》)

〔译文〕孟子说:"希望尊贵是人们共同的心理。每个人都有自己可尊贵的东西,只是不去考虑它罢了。别人所给的尊贵,不是真正值得尊贵的。"

Mencius said, "Highly valued things are what everybody desires. Each has his own valued things, only he does not think about it. Valued things given by others are not really valuable."

子曰:"贤哉,回也!一箪食,一瓢饮,在陋巷,人不堪其忧,回也不改其乐。贤哉,回也!"

(《论语·雍也》)

[译文]孔子说:"颜回多么有修养呀!一竹筐饭,一瓜瓢水,住在简陋的巷子里,别人受不了这种困苦,颜回却不改变他的快乐。颜回多么有修养呀!"

Confucius said, "Incomparable indeed was Yan Hui! A handful of rice to eat, a gourdful of water to drink, living in a shabby lane. Others would have found it unendurably depressing, but to Hui's cheerfulness it made no difference at all. Incomparable indeed was Yan Hui!"

孟子曰:"一箪食,一豆羹,得之则生,弗得则死,嘑尔而与之,行道之人弗受;蹴尔而与之,乞人不屑也。

(《孟子·告子上》)

〔译文〕孟子说："一筐饭,一碗汤,得着便能活下去,得不着便会死亡,如果呼喝着给与,过路的饿人也不会接受;如果脚踏过了再给与,就是乞丐也不愿意要。"

Mencius said,"A basket of rice or a bowl of soup can make a man live or die. If given by being shouted, a passing hungry man won't accept it . If given after the food being treaded, even a beggar won't accept it."

子曰:"奢则不孙,俭则固。与其不孙也,宁固。"

(《论语·述而》)

〔译文〕孔子说:"奢侈就显得傲慢,节俭就显得寒伧。与其傲慢,宁可寒伧。"

Confucius said, "Just as lavishness leads easily to presumption, so does frugality to meanness. Of the two I prefer the latter."

子曰:"人而无信,不知其可也。大车无輗,小车无軏,其何以行之哉?"

(《论语·为政》)

〔译文〕孔子说:"作为一个人,却不讲信用,不知他怎么可以立身处世。这就好比大车没有輗,小车没有軏,怎么能行走呢?"

Confucius said, "I really do not know how a man without faith could go on. Metaphorically, how can a cart or carriage be made to go without yoke or cross-bar?"

子曰:"如有周公之才之美,使骄且吝,其余不足观也已。"
(《论语·泰伯》)

〔译文〕孔子说:"一个人即使有周公那样美好的才能,而如果骄傲与吝啬,那其他方面也就不值得一看了。"

Confucius said, "If a man has gifts as wonderful as those of Duke Zhou, yet is arrogant and mean, the rest of him is of no account then."

子曰:"三军可夺帅也,匹夫不可夺志也。"
(《论语·子罕》)

〔译文〕孔子说:"三军的统帅可以被夺取,但是一个普通的男子汉,却不能强迫他放弃自己的主张。"

Confucius said, "The commander of the army may be carried off, but the will of a common man can not be made to change."

孟子曰:"柳下惠不以三公易其介。"

(《孟子·尽心上》)

〔译文〕孟子说:"柳下惠并不因为做了官而改变他的操守。"

Mencius said, "Liu Xiahui would not change his personal integrity for the high - ranking position."

子曰:"人无远虑,必有近忧。"

(《论语·卫灵公》)

〔译文〕孔子说:"一个人没有长远的考虑,事到跟前必有忧患。"

Confucius said, "If a man does not give thought to problems which are still distant, he will be worried by them when they come close at hand."

或曰:"以德报怨,何如?"子曰:"何以报德? 以直报怨,以德报德。"

(《论语·宪问》)

[译文]有人说:"用恩德来报答怨恨,这种做法怎么样?"孔子说:"用什么来报答恩德呢? 应该用正直来报答怨恨,用恩德来报答恩德。"

Someone said, "What about the saying 'meet resentment with kindness'?" Confucius said, "In that case, how is one to meet kindness? Rather, meet resentment with uprightness and meet kindness with kindness."

互乡难与言,童子见,门人惑。子曰:"与其进也,不与其退也,唯何甚? 人洁己以进,与其洁也,不保其往也。"

(《论语·述而》)

[译文]互乡这个地方的人难于交谈,但互乡的一位少年却得到孔子接见,弟子们感到疑惑不解。孔子说:"我赞许他的进步,不赞许他的退步,何必做得太过分! 人家把自己弄得干干净净而来,就应赞许他的干净,不要抓住他过去的污点不放。"

At Hu village, the people were difficult to talk to, so when a lad came to seek an interview and was received by Confucius, his disciples felt very confused. Confucius said, "We approve his striving for progress, not his tendency for retrogress. Why should we be too particular? If anyone strives for progress with the intention of purifying himself, we should approve this good intention; we should not fix our eyes upon his past."

子曰:"苗而不秀者有矣夫! 秀而不实者有矣夫!"

(《论语·子罕》)

〔译文〕孔子说:"庄稼出苗而不开花是有的吧! 开花而不结实也是有的吧!"

Confucius said, "There are shoots which can spring up but never flower; there are others which can flower but never bear fruit." (This probably refers to Yan Hui's early death.)

孟子曰:"恭者不侮人,俭者不夺人。侮夺人之君,惟恐不顺焉,恶得为恭俭? 恭俭岂可以声音笑貌为哉?"

(《孟子·离娄上》)

〔译文〕孟子说:"恭敬别人的人不会侮辱别人,自己节俭的人不会抢夺别人。有的国君专爱侮辱别人,抢夺别人,只怕别人不顺从自己,又如何能做到恭敬和节俭呢? 恭敬和节俭这两种美德怎么能凭说句好听的话,陪个笑脸就能办到的呢?"

Mencius said, "Those who are respectful to others would not insult; those who are frugal would not snatch others' things. Some monarchs like to insult and snatch for fear that others would not be obedient to them. How could they be respectful and frugal? Could it be said that the two virtues of respect and frugality can be achieved by speaking sweet words and showing a smiling face?"

孟子曰:"人有恒言,皆曰'天下国家'。天下之本在国,国之本在家,家之本在身。"

(《孟子·离娄上》)

〔译文〕孟子说:"大家有句口头话,都说'天下国家'。可见天下的基础是国,国的基础是家,而家的基础则是个人。"

Mencius said, "There is a pet phrase people all say, that is, 'the world, the country and the home'. It is thus evident that the basis of the world is the country, the basis of the country is the home and the basis of the home is the individual."

或谓孔子曰:"子奚不为政?"子曰:"《书》云:'孝乎惟孝,友于兄弟,施于有政。'是亦为政,奚其为为政?"

（《论语·为政》）

〔译文〕有人对孔子说："你为什么不当官参与政治呢？"孔子说："《尚书》上说：'既要孝敬父母，又能友爱兄弟'。把这种精神影响到社会上去，这也就是参与政治，为什么一定要做官才算参与政治呢？"

Someone said to Confucius, "Why don't you engage yourself in government?" Confucius said, "The Book of History says, 'Be filial, only be filial and friendly towards your brothers, and you will spread these qualities to government.' This too is to engage in government. Why does one have to hold office that he could be said to engage in government?"

孟子曰："人之有德慧术知者，恒存乎疢疾。独孤臣孽子，其操心也危，其虑患也深，故达。"

（《孟子·尽心上》）

〔译文〕孟子说："一个人之所以有道德、智慧，知识和本领，经常是由于遭到灾患而造成的。只有那种孤独的臣、庶孽之子，他们时常提高警惕，考虑灾患也深，所以才通达事理。"

Mencius said, "A person's virtue, wisdom, tactics and knowledge are often obtained under calamitous or unfavourable conditions. Only those lonely officials and sinful persons could often enhance their vigilance and think deeply on calamities, so they can understand things well."

子曰："笃信好学,守死善道。危邦不入,乱邦不居。天下有道则见,无道则隐。邦有道,贫且贱焉,耻也;邦无道,富且贵焉,耻也。"

(《论语·泰伯》)

〔译文〕孔子说："人要有坚定的信念和好学的精神,誓死去捍卫那些完善的治国做人的原则。危险的国家不要进入,有祸乱的国家不要去住。天下太平,就出来从政,不太平,就隐居起来。如果政治清明而自己贫贱,是耻辱;如果政治黑暗而自己富贵,也是耻辱。"

Confucius said, "A man should be of unwavering good faith, love learning and be ready to die for the good principles. He should not enter a state that pursues dangerous courses, nor stay in one where the people have rebelled. When the right way prevails under Heaven, then come out and take office; when it does not prevail, then go into hiding. When the right way prevails in your own land, count it a disgrace to be needy and obscure; when it does not prevail in your land, then count it a disgrace to be rich and honoured."

孟子曰:"耻之于人大矣,为机变之巧者,无所用耻焉。不耻不若人,何若人有?"

(《孟子·尽心上》)

〔译文〕孟子说:"羞耻之心对于人关系重大,干诡诈投机事情的人没有地方用得着羞耻。如果不以赶不上别人为羞耻,那又怎样能赶上别人呢?"

Mencius said, "The sense of shame is very important to people. Those who are cunning and opportunistic do not need to have the sense of shame. If you do not feel shameful for not catching up with others, then how can you catch up with others?"

孟子曰:"人不可以无耻,无耻之耻,无耻矣。"

(《孟子·尽心上》)

〔译文〕孟子说:"人不可以没有羞耻,不知羞耻的那种羞耻,才是真正的羞耻。"

Mencius said, "One should not have no sense of shame. It is a shame indeed when one does not know the sense of shame."

子曰:"人之生也直,罔之生也幸而免。"

(《论语·雍也》)

〔译文〕孔子说:"一个人能够生存在世界上是由于正直,不正直的人也可以生存,那是由于他侥幸地避免了祸害。"

Confucius said, "Man's life span depends upon his uprightness. He who goes on living without it escapes disaster only by good fortune."

孟子曰:"拱把之桐梓,人苟欲生之,皆知所以养之者。至于身,而不知所以养之者,岂爱身不若桐梓哉? 弗思甚也。"

(《孟子·告子上》)

〔译文〕孟子说:"一两把粗的桐树梓树,人们要想叫它生长起来,都知道怎样去培养它。至于本人,却不知道怎样去培养,难道爱自己还不如爱桐树梓树吗? 真是太不动脑筋了。"

Mencius said, "If people want a young sapling to grow up, they all know how to cultivate it. As for themselves, they do not know how to develop. Could it be said that they love themselves less than they love the sapling? They really don't think hard."

子曰:"巧言乱德。小不忍,则乱大谋。"

（《论语·卫灵公》）

[译文]孔子说:"花言巧语就会败坏道德。小事不能忍耐,就会乱了大事。"

Confucius said, "Sweet words may make virtue degenerate. Slight impatience may spoil great goals."

子曰:"士而怀居,不足以为士矣。"

（《论语·宪问》）

[译文]孔子说:"读书的人如果贪图安逸,那就不配做读书人了。"

Confucius said, "A scholar who prefers his own ease at home is no scholar at all."

孔子曰:"益者三乐,损者三乐。乐节礼乐,乐道人之善,乐多贤友,益矣。乐骄乐,乐佚游,乐宴乐,损矣。"

（《论语·季氏》）

[译文]孔子说:"有益的快乐有三种,有害的快乐也有三种。以保持礼乐适当得体为快乐,以宣扬别人的长处为快乐,以多交贤良的朋友为快乐,这是有益的。以尊贵骄傲为快乐,

以游荡忘返为快乐,以大吃大喝为快乐,这是有害的。"

Confucius said, "There are three types of pleasure that are profitable and three types that are harmful. The pleasure got from keeping to the proprieties of rites and music, the pleasure got from propagating others' strong points and the pleasure of having many friends of high caliber, are profitable. But pleasures got from conceit, from idle gadding about and from eating and drinking, are harmful."

孟子曰:"人之易其言也,无责耳矣。"

(《孟子·离娄上》)

〔译文〕孟子说:"如果一个人把什么话都轻易地说出口,那他就不足责备了。"

Mencius said, "If a person rashly speaks everything out, he is not worth reproaching."

子曰:"乡愿,德之贼也。"

(《论语·阳货》)

〔译文〕孔子说:"那种好好先生,是道德的败坏者呀。"

Confucius said, "The goody – goody people spoil the true virtue."

子曰:"道听途说,德之弃也。"

(《论语·阳货》)

〔译文〕孔子说:"在路上听到传言便到处去传播,这是对德行的背弃呀!"

Confucius said, "To spread what you have heard on the way is to abandon your virtue."

孟子曰:"人之患,在好为人师。"

(《孟子·离娄上》)

〔译文〕孟子说:"一个人的祸害,在于他喜欢当别人的老师。"

Mencius said, "One's trouble lies in liking to be a master to others."

孟子曰:"有不虞之誉,有求全之毁。"

(《孟子·离娄上》)

〔译文〕孟子说:"有料想不到的赞扬,也有过份苛刻的诋毁。"

Mencius said, "A person might receive unexpected praises as well as suffer excessively harsh slanders."

子曰:"岁寒,然后知松柏之后凋也。"

（《论语·子罕》）

〔译文〕孔子说:"天冷了,才知道松柏树是最后凋零的。"

Confucius said, "Only when the weather turns cold, do we see that the pine and cypress are the last to fade."

达巷党人曰:"大哉孔子! 博学而无所成名。"子闻之,谓门弟子曰:"吾何执? 执御乎? 执射乎? 吾执御矣。"

（《论语·子罕》）

〔译文〕达巷的一个人说:"孔子真伟大! 他学问渊博,但可惜没有足以树立名声的专长。"孔子听了这话,对学生们说:"我该专心于什么技艺呢? 驾车呢? 还是射箭呢? 我还是驾车吧。"

A man of Daxiang said, "Great indeed is Confucius! His learning is wide and profound, but there is nothing for which he is particularly renowned." Confucius, hearing of it, said to his disciples, "What shall I take up? Shall I take up chariot - driving? Or shall it be archery? I think I will take up driving (the humblest of the six arts)."

子曰:"若圣与仁,则吾岂敢?抑为之不厌,诲人不倦,则可谓云尔已矣。"公西华曰:"正唯弟子不能学也。"

(《论语·述而》)

〔**译文**〕孔子说:"如果说到圣和仁,那我怎么敢当?我不过是学习和工作总不厌烦,教诲别人总不疲倦,不过如此而已。"公西华说:"这正是我们学生学不到的。"

Confucius said, "I make no claim to be a sage or to be a virtuous man; but it can be said of me that I have made unwearying effort to learn and unflagging patience in teaching others." Upon this Gong Xihua said, "This is what we disciples are not able to learn."

孔子曰:"圣则吾不能,我学不厌而教不倦也。"

(《孟子》·公孙丑上)

〔译文〕孔子说:"圣人,我做不到,我只不过学习不知满足,教人不嫌疲倦罢了。"

Confucius said, "Divine sage, I can not be! It can only be said of me that I have made unwearing effort to learn and unflagging patience in teaching others."

子曰:"默而识之,学而不厌,诲人不倦,何有于我哉?"
(《论语·述而》)

〔译文〕孔子说:"把所见所闻默默记在心里,学习起来从不感到厌烦,教别人从不感到疲倦,这些事情我哪一点做得到呢?"

Confucius said, "To take note of things in silence, to retain curiosity in learning, to teach and never get wearied of it—to which of these can I make any claim?"

太宰问于子贡曰:"夫子圣者与?何其多能也?"子贡曰:"固天纵之将圣,又多能也。"

子闻之,曰:"太宰知我乎!吾少也贱,故多能鄙事。君子多乎哉?不多也。"

(《论语·子罕》)

〔译文〕太宰向子贡问道："孔老先生是圣人吗？他为什么这样多才多艺呢？"子贡说："这本是上天让他当圣人，又使他多才多艺。"

孔子听后说，"太宰哪里了解我呢？我小时穷苦，因此学会了不少鄙贱的技艺。一般的君子会有这么多的技艺吗？那是不会的。"

The Prime Minister asked Zi Gong, "Is your Master a sage? Why does he know so many trades?" Zi Gong replied, "It was Heaven that intended him to become a sage and be able to know many trades." When Confucius heard of this, he said, "How does the Prime Minister know me? When I was young I was poor, hence, I learned to do many practical things. Does a gentleman possess so many trades? No!"

子曰："吾有知乎哉？无知也。有鄙夫问于我，空空如也。我叩其两端而竭焉。"

（《论语·子罕》）

〔译文〕孔子说："我有知识吗？我没有知识。有一个乡下人问我，我对他的问题本来一无所知。我从他那个问题的正反两个方面加以盘问，才得到答案，然后尽量地告诉他。"

Confucius said, "Am I a learned man? No! A lowly peasant once asked me a question of which I was ignorant. I thrashed the matter out by studying the two sides of it and then told him all I knew about it."

子谓子贡曰:"女与回也孰愈?"对曰:"赐也何敢望回? 回也闻一以知十,赐也闻一以知二。"子曰:"弗如也;吾与女弗如也。"

(《论语·公冶长》)

〔译文〕孔子对子贡说:"你和颜回相比,谁更强一些呢?"子贡回答道:"我怎么敢和颜回相比呢? 他听到一件事,能联想到十件事;我听到一件事,只能联想到两件事。"孔子说:"你是赶不上他,你和我都赶不上他。"

Confucius said to Zi Gong, "Who is the better, you or Yan Hui?" He replied, "How can I be compared with Hui? On being taught one thing, he can be able to deduce ten other things, while I can only deduce two." Confucius said, "You are not as good as him. Neither you nor I am as good as him."

樊迟请学稼,子曰:"吾不如老农。"请学为圃,曰:"吾不如老圃。"

(《论语·子路》)

〔译文〕樊迟向孔子请教学种庄稼。孔子说:"我不如老农民。"樊迟又请教学种菜。孔子说:"我不如老菜农。"

Fan Chi asked Confucius to teach him about farming, Confucius said, "You had better consult some old farmer." He asked to be taught about gardening. Confucius said, "You had better go to some old vegetable – gardener."

孟子曰:"子路,人告之以有过,则喜。禹闻善言,则拜。"

（《孟子·公孙丑上》）

〔译文〕孟子说:"子路,别人把他的过失告诉他,他就高兴。禹听到善言,就给人家施礼。"

Mencius said, "When others told Zi Lu his faults, he would be glad. When Emperor Yu heard somebody express a good opinion, he would salute him."

子曰:"孟之反不伐。奔而殿,将入门,策其马,曰:'非敢后也,马不进也。'"

（《论语·雍也》）

〔译文〕孔子说:"孟之反不夸耀自己。他在打仗败退时留在最后作掩护,将要进入城门时,鞭打着他的马,说:'不是我敢于留在后面,是马不肯快走啊!'"

Confucius said, "Meng Zhifan is not a boaster. In the flight
from the enemy he was the last to flee. But when his men were
about to enter the gateway of their own city, he whipped his
horse and said, 'It isn't courage that makes me last, it is my
horse that could not gallop fast enough.'"

教育篇第四

BOOK Ⅳ EDUCATION

子适卫,冉有仆。子曰:"庶矣哉!"
冉有曰:"既庶矣,又何加焉?"曰:"富之。"
曰:"既富矣,又何加焉?"曰:"教之。"

(《论语·子路》)

〔译文〕孔子到了卫国,弟子冉有给他驾着车子。孔子说:"人口好稠密啊!"

冉有问:"人口多了,该怎么办呢?"孔子回答:"使他们富裕起来。"

冉有接着又问:"已经富裕了,又该怎么办呢?"孔子回答:"教育他们。"

When Confucius went to Wei, Ran You drove cart for him. "What a large population!" Confucius said. "Since the people are already numerous, what more would you do next?" Ran You asked. "Enrich them," was the reply. "And then what comes after they have become rich?" Confucius said, "Educate them."

孟子曰:"仁言不如仁声之入人深也,善政不如善教之得民也。善政,民畏之;善教,民爱之。善政得民财,善教得民心。"

《孟子·尽心上》）

〔译文〕孟子说："仁德的言语不如仁德的音乐使人感受深，良好的政治不如良好的教育能得到民心。良好的政治只能使百姓害怕；而良好的教育却能使百姓爱戴。良好的政治能得到百姓的财富，良好的教育却能得到百姓的心。"

Mencius said, "Virtuous music moves people more deeply than virtuous words; good education gets more support from the people than good politics. The common people are afraid of good politics but fond of good education. People's wealth can be obtained by good politics, but their hearts can be won only by education."

孟子曰："人之有道也，饱食、暖衣、逸居而无教，则近於禽兽。"

《孟子·滕文公上》）

〔译文〕孟子说："人有为人的道理。吃饱了、穿暖了、住得安逸了而如果没有教育，那就和禽兽差不多。"

Mencius said, "A man has his own principle of living. If he has enough to eat, warm clothes to wear, a comfortable house to live in, but receives no education, then he will be almost the same as an animal."

子曰:"爱之,能无劳乎? 忠焉,能勿诲乎?"

(《论语·宪问》)

〔译文〕孔子说:"父母爱子,怎能不叫他们勤劳呢? 臣忠于君,君又怎么不教诲他们呢?"

Confucius said, "How can they exact no effort from their child if they truly love him? How can the monarch refrain from instructing his ministers if they are truly loyal to him?"

孟子曰:"庠者,养也;校者,教也;序者,射也。夏曰校,殷曰序,周曰庠,学则三代共之,皆所以明人伦也。人伦明于上,小民亲于下。有王者起,必来取法。是为王者师也。"

(《孟子·滕文公上》)

〔译文〕孟子说:"庠,是教养的意思;校,是教诲的意思;序,是陈列的意思。夏代的地方学校叫校,殷代的地方学校叫序,周代的地方学校叫庠,至于大学,三代都叫学,它们的目的都是要阐明人与人之间的相互关系和行为准则。上层贵族明确了人与人的关系及行为准则,下层百姓会自然亲密地团结在一起。如果有圣王兴起,一定会来学习仿效。这便可做帝王的老师了。"

Mencius said, "*yang* means training; *xiao* means teaching; *xu* means displaying (education by displaying). The local school was called *xiao* in the Xia Dynasty; it was called *xu* in the Yin Dynasty; and it was called *yang* in the Zhou Dynasty. As to the university, all the three dynasties called it *xue*. The purpose of all these institutions was to teach people understand the ethical relations between people. If the upper-class nobles understand those ethical relations, the low-class common people would be closely united. If a sage emperor is rising, he must come to learn and imitate this, thus the scholars become the sage emperor's teachers."

子曰:"有教无类。"

(《论语·卫灵公》)

〔译文〕孔子说:"有求教于我的,我都教育,不管是什么人。"

Confucius said, "Instruction recognizes no castes."

孟子曰:"中也养不中,才也养不才,故人乐有贤父兄也。"

(《孟子·离娄下》)

〔译文〕孟子说:"道德品质好的人来教育薰陶道德品质不

好的人,有才能的人来教育薰陶那些没有才能的人,所以人人都喜欢有个好父兄来教育自己。”

Mencius said, "Those who have high moral standard can teach those who have low moral standard and those who have abilities can teach those who do not have abilities; so everyone likes to have a good father or a good elder brother to teach oneself."

公孙丑曰:“君子之不教子,何也?”

孟子曰:“势不行也。教者必以正;以正不行,继之以怒。继之以怒,则反夷矣。‘夫子教我以正,夫子未出于正也’。则是父子相夷也。父子相夷,则恶矣。古者易子而教之,父子之间不责善。责善则离,离则不祥,莫大焉。”

(《孟子·离娄上》)

〔译文〕公孙丑问:“君子不亲自教育儿子,这是为什么?”

孟子回答;“因为情势行不通。教育一定要用正理正道;父亲教儿子用正理正道不行时,接着来的是忿怒。一忿怒,那就伤感情了。儿子会说‘你教我正理正道,可你不按正理正道做’,这就是父子之间互相伤感情了。父子一伤感情,那就很不好。古人交换着对儿子进行教育,使父子之间不因求好而相责备。因为求其好会使父子隔阂,父子之间有了隔阂,是最不好的一件事。”

Gongsun Chou asked, "Why doesn't the gentleman teach his own son?"

Mencius said, "This is because the situation is difficult. Education must be carried out with correctness. If there is no good effect after the father has taught his son with correctness, the father's anger comes. Anger would do harm to the feelings. The son would say, 'You teach me to be correct, but you do not behave correctly.' Thus the mutual feelings are harmed. It is very bad to harm the feelings between father and son, The ancient people educate each other's sons for exchange to avoid mutual reproaching and harming feelings between father and son. Father and son may reproach each other because of seeking goodness. This mutual reproaching would lead to estrangement; and the estrangement between father and son is the worst thing."

孟子曰："教亦多术矣，予不屑之教诲也者，是亦教诲之而已矣。"

(《孟子·告子下》)

〔译文〕孟子说："教育人有许多方式。如果我认为不值得而不去教育他，这也是一种教诲的方式。"

Mencius said, "There are many ways to teach people. If I think one is not worth my effort to teach him, this is also a way of teaching."

孟子曰:"君子之所以教者五:有如时雨化之者,有成德者,有达才者,有答问者,有私淑艾者。此五者,君子之所以教也。"

(《孟子·尽心上》)

〔译文〕孟子说:"君子教育人的方式有五种:有像及时雨那样浇灌万物的,有成全别人的品德的,有培养别人的才能的,有解答别人疑问的,还有以流风余韵传下来,供后人学习的。这五种便是君子教育人的方法。"

Mencius said, "The gentlemen have five ways to educate people. Some exert their influence on people like the timely rain falling on plants; some help people to achieve their good moral characters; some train people's abilities; some answer others' questions; and some leave a good name for posterity to learn from. These are the five ways that the gentlemen use to educate people."

子曰:"性相近也,习相远也。"

(《论语·阳货》)

〔译文〕孔子说:"人的性情本来是互相接近的,但由于习俗的不同才渐渐地变远了。”

Confucius said, " In our natures we approximate one
another; habits put us further and further apart."

孟子曰:"居移气,养移体,大哉居乎!"

(《孟子·尽心上》)

〔译文〕孟子说:"环境能改变气质,奉养能改变体质,环境
真是太重要了。"

Mencius said, " The enviroment can change one's
temperaments, feeding and waiting upon can change one's
physique. So important is the enviroment!"

孟子曰:"富岁,子弟多赖;凶岁,子弟多暴,非天之降才尔
殊也,其所以陷溺其心者然也。"

(《孟子·告子上》)

〔译文〕孟子说:"丰收年成,年青人多表现懒散;灾荒年
成,年青人多表现强暴,这并不是天生的资质有所不同,而是
由于环境把他们的心情变坏了的缘故。"

Mencius said, "In years of bumper harvest, the young are

often lazy; while in years of famine, the young are often violent. Not that their natures are different, but that the enviroments change their heart for the worse."

孟子曰:"虽有天下易生之物也,一日暴之,十日寒之,未有能生者也。"

(《孟子·告子上》)

〔译文〕孟子说:"即使有一种最容易生长的植物,晒它一天,再冻它十天,没有能够再生长的。"

Mencius said, "Even if there is a kind of plant that can grow up most easily, it can not grow any more with one day's drying in the sun and ten day's freezing in the cold."

子曰:"饱食终日,无所用心,难矣哉! 不有博奕者乎? 为之,犹贤乎已。"

(《论语·阳货》)

〔译文〕孔子说:"整天吃饱了饭,却无所事事,不行的呀! 不是有下奕棋的游戏吗? 干干那也比闲着好。"

Confucius said, "Those who do nothing all day but cram themselves with food are no good! Are there not games such as draughts? Playing them would surely be better than doing nothing at all."

子曰：“我非生而知之者，好古，敏以求之者也。”

（《论语·述而》）

[译文]孔子说：“我不是一生下来就有知识的人，而是善于向古人学习，遇到问题善于勤奋敏捷地去探求的一个人。”

Confucius said, "I wasn't born with innate knowledge. By learning from the ancients, I sought it through diligence."

子入太庙，每事问。或曰：“孰谓鄹人之子知礼乎？入太庙，每事问。”子闻之，曰：“是礼也。”

（《论语·八佾》）

[译文]孔子到了周公庙，每件事都要发问。有人便说：“谁说叔梁纥的这个儿子知道礼？你看他进了太庙，什么都问。”孔子听了这番话后却说：“这正是知礼啊！”

When Confucius entered the Grand Temple he asked questions about everything there. Someone said, "How can it be said that the son of Shu Lianghe (father of Confucius) knows the rites? Every time he is present he asks about everything!" When this was reported to Confucius he said, "This is just the rite."

子曰:"十室之邑,必有忠信如丘焉,不如丘之好学也。"

（《论语·公冶长》）

[译文]孔子说:"在一个仅有十户人家的小村子里,一定能找到和我孔丘一样忠厚信实的人,只是不如我孔丘好学罢了。"

Confucius said, "In any hamlet of ten households, you may be sure of finding someone who is quite as loyal and true as I, but I doubt if you could find anyone who equals my love of learning."

叶公问孔子于子路,子路不对。子曰:"女奚不曰,其为人也,发奋忘食,乐以忘忧,不知老之将至云尔。"

（《论语·述而》）

[译文]叶公向子路询问孔子是怎样的人,子路不知道怎样回答。孔子说:"你为什么不这样说,他的为人呀,发愤用起功来,便忘记了吃饭,得到学习里面的快乐,连忧愁也忘记了。明明自己老了还不知道,如此而已。"

The Duke of Ye asked about Confucius. Zi Lu made no reply. Confucius said to him afterwards, "Why didn't you say: He is a man whose zeal for work is such that he forgets to eat, whose happiness in his pursuit of knowledge is so great that he forgets his trouble and does not perceive old age stealing upon him."

子曰:"……敏而好学,不耻下问。"

（《论语·公冶长》）

〔译文〕孔子说:"……思想敏捷而又爱好学习,谦虚下问而又不以为耻。

Confucius said, "……Be keen on and fond of learning, seek advice modestly from anyone, including those who are even lower than oneself."

子曰:"君子食无求饱,居无求安,敏于事而慎于言,就有道而正焉,可谓好学也已。"

（《论语·学而》）

〔译文〕孔子说:"君子饮食不要求饱足,居住不要求舒适,办事敏捷,说话谨慎,向有道德的人学习而改正自己的缺点,这样就可以说是好学的人了。"

Confucius said, "A gentleman does not seek satiety at table or ease at home; he is diligent in work and cautious in speech; he turns to those of virtue so as to rectify himself. Such a man may well be said as being eager to learn."

子曰:"学如不及,犹恐失之。"

(《论语·泰伯》)

〔译文〕孔子说:"学习起来总感到自己好像没学好似的,学到以后,还恐怕再失掉。"

Confucius said, "Study as if you were never to master it; as if you were in fear of losing what you have learned."

子曰:"吾尝终日不食,终夜不寝,以思,无益,不如学也。"

(《论语·卫灵公》)

〔译文〕孔子说:"我曾经整天不吃饭,整夜不睡觉,反复思考,却没有益处,不如去学习。"

Confucius said, "I once spent a whole day without food and a whole night without sleep, in order to meditate. I found no advantage in it. It is better to learn."

子曰:"……好仁不好学,其蔽也愚;好知不好学,其蔽也荡;好信不好学,其蔽也贼;好直不好学,其蔽也绞;好勇不好学,其蔽也乱;好刚不好学,其蔽也狂。"

(《论语·阳货》)

〔译文〕孔子说:"……如果只喜欢仁德不喜欢学习的话,那就会被人愚弄;如果爱耍聪明不爱学习的话,他的行为便会放荡;如果只知道信实不喜欢学习的话,那就会被人利用,坏了大事,反倒害了自己;如果只喜爱正直不喜欢学习的话,那么就会说话尖刻,容易得罪人;如果只是勇敢而不喜欢学习的话,那就容易捣乱闯祸;如果只是爱刚强而不爱学习的话,那就容易行为轻狂,胆大妄为。"

Confucius said, "Love of goodness without Love of learning degenerates into silliness. Love of wisdom without love of learning degenerates into presumption. love of honesty without love of learning degenerates into being easily used and harming oneself. love of uprightness without love of learning degenerates into rudeness. love of daring without love of learning degenerates into turbulence. love of firmness without love of learning degenerates into arrogance."

子曰:"三人行,必有我师焉。择其善者而从之,其不善者而改之。"

(《论语·述而》)

〔译文〕孔子说:"三个人在一起走路,其中一定有人可以做我的老师。我选择他们的优点供自己学习,把他们的缺点作为自己的借鉴而改掉。"

Confucius said, "When three of us are walking together, I am sure to have a teacher. I'd select his merits to follow, and his demerits to correct myself."

子曰:"学而时习之,不亦说乎? 有朋自远方来,不亦乐乎? 人不知而不愠,不亦君子乎?"

(《论语·学而》)

〔译文〕孔子说:"对学得的知识按时去温习,不也很高兴么? 有志同道合的人从远方来,不也很快乐么? 人家对我不了解而我却不生气,不也是君子么?"

Confucius said, "To learn and at due times to repeat what one has learned, is that not after all a pleasure? To have friends come to you from afar, is that not after all delightful? To remain unsoured when others do not know of you, is that not after all what is expected of a gentleman?"

子曰:"温故而知新,可以为师矣。"

(《论语·为政》)

[译文]孔子说:"温习过去所学的知识,能有新体会,新见解,这样就可以当老师了。"

Confucius said, "Acquire new knowledge while thinking over the old, and you may become a teacher of others."

孟子曰:"博学而详说之,将以反说约也。"

(《孟子·离娄下》)

[译文]孟子说:"先要广博地学习,详细地解说,(在融会贯通之后)再反回到简略地述说大意的位置。"

Mencius said, "One should first learn extensively and explain in detail what he has learned, (after a complete mastery of the subject) then return to the position of briefly telling the general idea."

子曰:"学而不思则罔,思而不学则殆。"

(《论语·为政》)

〔译文〕孔子说:"如果只学习不思考,就要陷入迷罔之中;如果只思考不学习,问题仍然疑惑不解。"

Confucius said, "He who learns but does not think is lost. He who thinks but does not learn still remains puzzled."

子曰:"盖有不知而作之者,我无是也。多闻,择其善者而从之;多见而识之;知之次也。"

（《论语·述而》）

〔译文〕孔子说:"似乎有一种自己不懂却凭空造作的人,我没有这个毛病。多听各种意见,选择其中好的来学习;多看各种事情,牢牢地记在心里;这样学来的知识是仅次于生来就知道的知识。"

Confucius said, "There may well be those who can do without knowledge; but I am certainly not one of them. To hear much, pick out what is good and follow it, to see much and remember it; the knowledge gained this way is second only to that innate in man."

子曰:"知之者不如好之者,好之者不如乐之者。"

（《论语·雍也》）

〔译文〕孔子说:"(对于任何学问和事业,)懂得它的人不如喜爱它的人,喜爱它的人不如以它为乐的人。"

Confucius said, "(for any knowledge and profession) To prefer it is better than only to know it. To delight in it is better than merely to prefer it."

子曰:"由,诲女知之乎! 知之为知之,不知为不知,是知也。"

(《论语·为政》)

〔译文〕孔子说:"仲由,我教给你关于学知识的道理。知道就是知道,不知道就是不知道,这才是真正的知道呢。"

Confucius said, "Zhong You, I shall teach you what knowledge is! When you know a thing, say that you know it; when you do not know a thing, admit that you do not know it. That is true knowledge."

孟子曰:"羿之教人射,必志于彀;学者亦必志于彀。大匠诲人必以规矩,学者亦必以规矩。"

(《孟子·告子上》)

〔译文〕孟子说:"羿教人射箭时,一定把弓拉满;学射的人也一定要把弓拉满。有名的木工教徒弟时,一定按照规矩,学习的人也必须按照一定的规矩。"

Mencius said, "When Yi teaches others shooting, he certainly draws the bow in full; the learner also has to draw the bow in full. When a well-known carpenter teaches his apprentice, he certainly teaches according to the rules; and the learner also has to learn accordingly."

孟子谓高子曰:"山径之蹊,间介然用之而成路;为间不用,则茅塞之矣。今茅塞子之心矣。"

(《孟子·尽心下》)

〔译文〕孟子对高子说:"山坡上的小路只有一点点宽,经常去走它,便成为路;只要有一些时间不去走它,又会被茅草堵塞了。现在茅草也把你的心堵塞了。"

Mencius said to Master Gao, "Even the mountain path is very narrow, it can become a road if you often walk on it. But if you don't walk on it for some time, it will be blocked up by the cogongrass again. Now the cogongrass has blocked up your heart."

孟子曰:"今夫奕之为数,小数也;不专心致志,则不得也。

奕秋,通国之善奕者也。使奕秋诲二人奕,其一人专心致志,惟奕秋之为听。一人虽听之,一心以为有鸿鹄将至,思援弓缴而射之,虽与之俱学,弗若之矣。为是其智弗若与? 曰:非然也。"

(《孟子·告子上》)

〔译文〕孟子说:"例如下棋,这只是一种小技术。如果不一心一意,也学不好。奕秋是全国的下棋能手。假使让奕秋教两个人下棋,一个人一心一意,完全听奕秋的话。另一个人表面上虽然听,心里却一直想着天上正飞来一只天鹅,想拿起弓来去射它。他虽然和那个人一道学习,但成绩却不如人家。是因为他不如人家聪明吗? 自然不是的。"

Mencius said, "Playing chess, for example, is a small skill, but you can not learn it well if you do not learn it wholeheartedly. Suppose Yiqiu, the well-known chess player in the country, is teaching two persons to play chess at the same time. One is learning heart and soul, remembering Yiqiu's teaching completely. The other seems to be listening to Yiqiu's teaching, but actually he is thinking that a swan in the sky is flying to him and he wants to take a bow to shoot it. Although he is learning in the same way as the other, his achievements are not as good. Is it because he is not as clever as the other? Of course not."

孟子曰:"大匠不为拙工改废绳墨,羿不为拙射变其彀率。君子引而不发,跃如也。中道而立,能者从之。"

(《孟子·尽心上》)

〔译文〕孟子说:"高明的工匠不会因为拙劣的工人而改变或废弃自己做工的规矩,名射手羿也不会因为拙劣的射手变更拉开弓的标准。君子教导别人好像张满了弓却不发箭,做出跃跃欲试的样子。他在正确的道路上站立,有能力的便跟随而来。"

Mencius said "The brilliant craftsman would not abandon his rules of work because of the clumsy workers. The well-known shooter Yi would not change his standards of drawing the bow because of the clumsy shooters. When the gentleman teaches others, he shows them how to do without doing it for them. He sticks to the correct way and those who are competent can follow him."

子绝四:毋意,毋必,毋固,毋我。

(《论语·子罕》)

〔译文〕孔子坚决杜绝下面四种毛病:不凭空猜测,不绝对肯定,不抱泥固执,不自以为是。

There are four things that Confucius always tried to guard

against: He made no conjectures nor absolute certainty; he was never obstinate, never egotistic.

子路问:"闻斯行诸?"子曰:"有父兄在,如之何其闻斯行之?"

冉有问:"闻斯行诸?"子曰:"闻此行之。"

公西华曰:"由也问闻斯行诸,子曰'有父兄在';求也问闻斯行诸,子曰:'闻斯行之'。赤也惑,敢问。"子曰:"求也退,故进之;由也兼人,故退之。"

(《论语·先进》)

〔译文〕子路问:"听到以后就干起来吗?"孔子回答:"有你父亲和哥哥活着,怎么能听到就干起来呢?"

冉有问:"听到以后就干起来吗?"孔子回答:"你听到以后就干起来吧。"

公西华说:"仲由问你听到以后就干起来吗,你回答'有父亲和哥哥活着,不能听到就干起来。'冉求向您问起同一问题时,您却回答'听到以后就干起来。'我对这种回答不解,大胆地向您提出疑问。"

孔子说:"冉求平日做事过于谨慎,所以我鼓励他遇事大胆干。而仲由胆量太大,做起事来往往不加考虑,所以我要适当地抑止他一下。"

Zi Lu saked, "Shall I put what I have heard into practice immediately?" Confucius said, "How can you do so while your father and elder brother are still alive?" Ran You asked the same question, however, Confucius replied, "Put it into practice immediately." Gong Xihua then spoke up, "The replies you have just given puzzled me and I beg for an explanation." Confucius said, "Ran is apt to hang back, so I press him on; Zi Lu is bold and careless, so I hold him back."

孟子曰:"有为者辟若掘井,掘井九轫而不及泉,犹为弃井也。"

(《孟子·尽心上》)

〔译文〕孟子说:"做事情好比掏井,如果掏到六七丈深还不见泉水的话,便仍然是个废井。"

Mencius said, "To do a thing is just like digging a well. If you have dug about twenty meters deep into the ground without seeing the wellspring, it is still an abandoned well."

孟子曰:"梓匠轮舆能与人规矩,不能使人巧。"

(《孟子·尽心下》)

〔译文〕孟子说:"木匠或专做车子的匠人能够把制作的办法标准传授给别人,却不能使人一定学到高明的技巧。"

Confucius said, "Set your heart upon the right way, support yourself by virtue, lean upon benevolence, seek distraction in the six arts (music, archery and the like)."

子曰："兴于《诗》,立于礼,成于乐。"

（《论语·泰伯》）

[译文]孔子说："诗篇使人振奋精神,礼仪使人在社会上站得住脚跟,音乐使人陶冶情操。"

Confucius said, "People are inspired by poetry, then given a firm footing by the study of rites, and finally perfected by music."

子曰："小子何莫学夫诗？诗,可以兴,可以观,可以群,可以怨。迩之事父,远之事君;多识于鸟兽草木之名。"

（《论语·阳货》）

[译文]孔子说："学生们为什么不学诗呢？学诗,可以培养联想力,可以开扩人的眼界,可以懂得人世交往的方法,可以学得如何表达怨恨。近则可以用诗中的道理事奉父母,远则可以用诗中的道理事奉君主;还可以多知道一些鸟兽草木的名称。"

Confucius said, "My pupils, why do none of you study The Poems? Through The Poems minds can be aroused, a point of vantage gained, sociability exercised, resentments expressed. They may be used at home in the service of one's parents; outside, in the service of one's prince. Moreover, they will widen your acquaintance with the names of birds, beasts, plants and trees."

子曰:"诗三百,一言以蔽之,曰:'思无邪'。"
（《论语·为政》）

[译文]孔子说:"《诗》三百篇,用一句话来概括,就是'思想纯正'。"

Confucius said, "If I have to take a single phrase to sum up the Three Hundred Songs, I would say, 'Let there be no evil in your thoughts.'"

陈亢问于伯鱼曰:"子亦有异闻乎?"对曰:"未也。尝独立,鲤趋而过庭。曰:'学《诗》乎?'对曰:'未也。''不学《诗》,无以言。'鲤退而学诗。他日,又独立,鲤趋而过庭。曰:'学礼乎?'对曰:'未也。''不学礼,无以立。'鲤退而学礼。闻斯二者。"

陈亢退而喜曰:"问一得三,闻诗,闻礼,又闻君子之远其子也。"

(《论语·季氏》)

〔译文〕陈亢向孔子的儿子伯鱼问道:"你在老师那里听到什么特别的教导吗?"伯鱼回答说:"没有。我父亲有一天曾独自在庭院里站着,我快步走过。他问我说:'学诗了没有?'我回答说:'没有。'他说:'不学诗,就不善于说话。'于是我便回来学诗。又有一天,他独自站在院中,我快步从庭院走过。他又问我:'你学礼了吗?'我回答说:'没有。'他说:'不学礼,就不能立身处世。'于是我便退回来学礼。我只听到这两件事。"陈亢回去高兴地说:"我问了一件事,却知道了三件事:知道学诗、学礼的重要,也知道君子不偏爱自己的儿子。"

Chen Kang asked Bo Yu, "Have you ever received any different teaching from your father?" He replied, "No. But once, when I was passing hurriedly through the court yard, I met my father standing alone, and he said, 'Have you studied The Poems?' I replied, 'Not yet.' He said, 'If you do not study The Poems, you won't be able to carry on a conversation.' Thereupon I withdrew and studied The Poems. Another day I met him again standing alone as I hastened through the court yard, and he said, 'Have you studied The Book of Rites?' I replied, 'Not yet.' He said, 'If you do not study The Book of Rites, you will never take your stand!' So I withdrew and studied The Book of Rites. These are the two pieces of instruction I have received from my father." Chen Kang went away rejoicing and said, "I asked about one thing and have learned three—something about The Poems, something about The Book of Rites, and also that a true gentleman has no prejudice in favour of his own son."

子谓伯鱼曰:"女为《周南》、《召南》矣乎? 人而不为《周南》、《召南》,其犹正墙面而立也与?"

(《论语·阳货》)

[译文]孔子对伯鱼说:"你学习《周南》、《召南》了吗? 一个人如果不学习《周南》、《召南》,那就好比正面向着墙壁站立一样(无法行走了)!"

Confucius said to Bo Yu, "Have you studied Zhou Nan and Shao Nan (the first two sections of The Poems)? He who has not even studied Zhou Nan and Shao Nan is as though he stood with his face pressed against a wall!"

子曰:"关雎,乐而不淫,哀而不伤。"

(《论语·八佾》)

[译文]孔子说:"《关雎》这首诗快乐而不放荡,忧愁而不悲伤。"(本诗写一个男子追求一个少女的忧思和喜悦。)

Confucius said, "The poem Guanjiu expresses joy not carried to the point of debauch, and grief not carried to the point of heart-break."(The poem begins by describing a lover's grief at being separated from his lady and ends by describing their joyful union.)

子曰："辞达而已矣。"

(《论语·卫灵公》)

〔译文〕孔子说："言辞能够把意思表达清楚就可以了。"

Confucius said, "It is enough that one's words express fully one's thought."

子在齐闻《韶》，三月不知肉味，曰："不图为乐之至于斯也。"

(《论语·述而》)

〔译文〕孔子在齐国听到《韶》乐时，好长时间吃肉不觉滋味，于是说："想不到欣赏音乐竟到了这般境界。"

When he was in Qi State Confucius heard the Shun's music and for three months did not know the taste of meat. He said, "I never thought that I could be lost in that music to such an extent."

子谓《韶》,"尽美矣,又尽善也。"谓《武》,"尽美矣,未尽善也。"

(《论语·八佾》)

[译文]孔子谈论《韶乐》时说:"美极了(可能指声音而言),而且好极了(可能指内容而言)。"谈到《武乐》时说:"美极了,但还不够好。"(《韶》是歌颂舜的乐曲,舜的帝位是尧"禅让"而来的,所以孔子说"尽善"。《武》是歌颂周武王的乐曲,周武王的帝位是用武力讨伐商纣夺来的,所以孔子说"未尽善"。)

Confucius spoke of the Shao music as being perfect beauty and at the same time perfect goodness; but of the Wu music as being perfect beauty, but not perfect goodness. (The Shao music mimed the peaceful accession of the legendary Emperor Shun; the War music mimed the accession by conquest of the Emperor Wu, who overthrew the Yin Dynasty.)

子语鲁大师乐曰:"乐其可知也:始作,翕如也;从之,纯如也,皦如也,绎如也,以成。"

(《论语·八佾》)

　　〔译文〕孔子把演奏音乐的过程讲给鲁国的太师听,说:"演奏音乐的过程是可以知道的:开始时,发音合奏;继续下去,音调和谐,明亮清晰,余音袅袅,然后结束。"

　　When talking to the Grand Master of the Lu State about music, Confucius said, "Music can be learned. It begins with a strict but violent unison. Soon the musicians are given more liberty, and the tone becomes purely harmonious, brilliant, consistent, right on to the end."

处世篇第五

BOOK Ⅴ CONDUCT ONESELF IN SOCIETY

孟子曰：“仁也者，人也。合而言之，道也。”

（《孟子·尽心下》）

〔译文〕孟子说：“仁的意思就是人。‘仁’和‘人’合起来说便是道。”

Mencius said, "Benevolence derives from humanity. 'Benevolence' plus 'humanity' is the doctrine."

子曰：“人能弘道，非道弘人。”

（《论语·卫灵公》）

〔译文〕孔子说：“人能够把道发扬光大，而道不能把人的各方面弘扬光大。”

Confucius said, "A man can develop the way, but there is no way that can develop a man."

子曰：“朝闻道，夕死可矣。”

（《论语·里仁》）

〔译文〕孔子说:"早上听到了真理,当天晚上死去都可以。"

Confucius said, "In the morning, I hear the truth; in the evening, I die content."

孟子曰:"天下有道,以道殉身;天下无道,以身殉道;未闻以道殉乎人者也。"

(《孟子·尽心上》)

〔译文〕孟子说:"天下政治清明,便全力推行道;政治黑暗,则不惜为卫道而死;从来没听说过以牺牲道来迁就王侯的。"

Mencius said, "A gentleman pursues truth when the government is upright and free from corruption, but he will not hesitate to die in defence of it when the government is fatuous and corrupt. I have never heard of anyone who will sacrifice truth to accommodate himself to some big figures."

子曰:"道不同,不相为谋。"

(《论语·卫灵公》)

〔译文〕孔子说:"持不同主张的人,不能在一起商讨问题。"

Confucius said, "Men who differ in their principles cannot take counsel with each other."

子曰:"可与共学,未可与适道;可与适道,未可与立;可与立,未可与权。"

(《论语·子罕》)

[译文]孔子说:"可以同他一道学习的人,未必可以同他一道去探求真理;可以同他一道去探求真理,却未必可以同他一道有所建树;可以同他一道有所建树,却未必可以同他一道通权达变。"

Confucius said, "There are some people with whom you may study together but you can hardly seek truth together with them; even if you may seek truth together with them, you won't be able to achieve anything with them; even if you may achieve something together with them , you won't be able to make adaptations together with them."

孟子曰:"身不行道,不行于妻子;使人不以道,不能行于妻子。"

(《孟子·尽心下》)

〔译文〕孟子曰:"本人不依道而行,道在妻子身上也行不通;使唤别人不依道而行,要去使唤妻子也不可能。"

Mencius said, "If one does not act according to principles, his principles do not work even on his wife. If one does not use others in accordance with priciples, these principles even can't be applied to his wife."

子曰:"邦有道,危言危行;邦无道,危行言孙。"

(《论语·宪问》)

〔译文〕孔子说:"国家政治清明,说话要正直,行为要正直;国家政治黑暗,行为要正直,但说话要随和谨慎。"

Confucius said, "When the right way prevails in the country, you may speak and act uprightly. When the right way does not prevail, let your acts be upright but your speech accommodating."

孟子曰:"夫道若大路然,岂难知哉? 人病不求耳。"

(《孟子·告子下》)

〔译文〕孟子说:"道就像大路一样,难道说是很难了解吗?

只怕人不去寻求罢了。"

Mencius said, "Truth is just like a road. Is it difficult to learn about it? No, the problem is that people are declined to persue it."

孟子曰:"是故诚者,天之道也;思诚者,人之道也。至诚而不动者,未之有也;不诚,未有能动者也。"

(《孟子·离娄上》)

[译文]孟子说:"所以诚是自然的规律;追求诚是做人的规律。极端诚心而不能使别人感动的事是没有的;而不诚心也没有能感动别人的。"

Mencius said, "So sincerity is the natural law; pursuing sincerity is the law of being a man. Nobody can not be moved by complete sincerity; and nobody can be moved by the lack of sincerity."

子在川上曰:"逝者如斯夫,不舍昼夜。"

(《论语·子罕》)

[译文]孔子站在河边上叹道:"消逝的时光如同河中的流水,日夜不停地向前流去。"

Standing by a stream, Confucius said, "Time goes on and on like the flowing water in the river, never ceasing day or night!"

子曰:"天何言哉? 四时行焉,百物生焉。天何言哉?"

(《论语·阳货》)

〔译文〕孔子说:"天说了些什么呢? 四季照样运行,万物照样生长。天又说了些什么呢?"

Confucius said, "Heaven says nothing! Yet the four seasons run their course and all things are produced. Heaven says nothing!"

季路问事鬼神。子曰:"未能事人,焉能事鬼?"曰:"敢问死。"曰:"未知生,焉知死?"

(《论语·先进》)

〔译文〕季路向孔子问起怎样服事鬼神的事。孔子说:"活人还不能服事,怎么能去服事鬼神呢?"季路又说:"我再大胆地向您问问死是怎么回事。"孔子说:"生的道理我还没弄明白,怎么能懂得死呢?"

Ji Lu asked about men's duty to spirits. Confucius said, "Before we are able to serve the living, how can we serve the spirits of the dead?" Ji Lu went on to ask about death. Confucius said, "Before we know what life is, how can we know what death is?"

　　子不语怪、力、乱、神。

(《论语·述而》)

　　〔译文〕孔子不随便谈论怪异,勇力,混乱和鬼神之类的事情。

Confucius never talked of prodigies(of nature), feats of strength, disorders(of nature) or spirits.

　　子张问:"十世可知也?"子曰:"殷因于夏礼,所损益可知也;周因于殷礼,所损益可知也;其或继周者,虽百世,可知也。"

(《论语·为政》)

　　〔译文〕子张问:"今后十代的礼仪制度可以知道吗?"孔子说:"殷朝承袭了夏朝的礼仪制度,它所废除和增加了什么是可以知道的;周朝承袭了殷朝的礼仪制度,它所废除和增加了什么是可以知道的;那么,继承周朝的某个朝代,既使在一百代以后,它的礼仪制度也是可以依次类推而知道的。"

Zi Zhang asked whether it was possible to know about things ten generations afterwards. Confucius said, "We know in what ways the Yin dynasty modified rites when they followed upon the Xia dynasty. We know in what ways the Zhou dynasty modified rites when they followed upon the Yin dynasty. Hence we can foretell the rites the successors of the Zhou dynasty will practise, even one hundred generations hence, it is possible by analogy to know their characteristics."

子贡问曰:"有一言而可以终身行之者乎?"子曰:"其恕乎! 己所不欲,勿施于人。"

(《论语·卫灵公》)

〔译文〕子贡问道:"有没有一句可以终身奉行的话呢?"孔子说:"大概就是恕吧! 凡是自己不愿意的事情,就不要强加到别人身上。"

Zi Gong asked, "Is there a single saying that one can act upon throughout one's life?" Confucius said, "Perhaps the word of Shu(forbearance), which means never to do to others what you would not like to do to you."

孟子曰:"贤者以其昭昭使人昭昭。今以其昏昏使人昭昭。"

(《孟子·尽心下》)

〔译文〕孟子说:"贤能的人一定是先使自己明白了,再使别人明白。今天的人自己还在糊涂,却用模模糊糊的东西去使别人明白。"

Mencius said, "The virtuous and competent people would undertand first, then let others understand. Some current people are confused themselves but force others to understand."

孟子曰:"非礼之礼,非义之义,大人弗为。"

(《孟子·离娄下》)

〔译文〕孟子说:"似是而非的礼,似是而非的义,有德行的人是不干的。"

Mencius said, "Virtuous people won't do anything that is not really ritual and righteous."

孟子曰:"无为其所不为,无欲其所不欲,如此而已矣。"

(《孟子·尽心上》)

〔译文〕孟子说:"不去干我所不愿干的事,不去要我不想要的东西,这样就可以了。"

Mencius said, "I am not going to do what I won't do and take what I don't like. That's all."

孟子曰:"知者无不知也,当务之为急;仁者无不爱也,急亲贤之为务。"

(《孟子·尽心上》)

〔译文〕孟子说:"聪明人没有不应该知道的,但最急迫的是要知道当前的重要工作;仁慈的人没有不爱的,但务必要爱亲人和贤者。"

Mencius said, "There is nothing that the wise man does not know, but the most urgent that he should know is the current important thing; There is no one that the benevolent man does not love, but he must love his parents and the virtuous people first."

公孙丑曰:"敢问夫子恶乎长?"

曰:"我知言,我善养吾浩然之气。"

"敢问何谓浩然之气?"

曰:"难言也。其为气也,至大至刚,以直养而无害,则塞于天地之间。其为气也,配义与道;无是,馁也。"

(《孟子·公孙丑上》)

〔**译文**〕公孙丑问道:"请问老师对哪方面擅长?"

孟子说:"我善于分析别人的言词,也善于培养我自己的浩然之气。"

公孙丑又问道:"请问什么叫做浩然之气呢?"

孟子说:"这就不好说明白了,那一种气,最伟大最刚强,如果用正义去培养它,不伤害它,它便充塞于天地四方。那种气必须与义和道配合起来,如果缺乏这一点,便没有力量了。"

Gong Sunchou asked, "What are you good at, sir?"

Mencius said, "I'm good at analysing others' words and fostering my own noble spirit."

Gong Sunchou asked again, "What does 'noble spirit' mean?"

Mencius said, "It's hard to express. But that kind of spirit is both great and unyielding. If it is fostered in a righteous way and not hurt, it will fill under heaven. The spirit must be combined with justice and truth.

It will be forceless without it."

子曰:"不逆诈,不亿不信,抑亦先觉者,是贤乎!"

(《论语·宪问》)

〔译文〕孔子说:"不预先怀疑别人欺诈,也不随意猜测别人不讲信用,然而却能及早觉察出这一切的人,才是贤人啊!"

Confucius said "The man who does not doubt about the deceit of others nor reckon upon promises not being kept but is conscious of both beforehand is really a sage!"

子曰:"二三子以我为隐乎? 吾无隐乎尔。吾无行而不与二三子者,是丘也。"

(《论语·述而》)

〔译文〕孔子说:"你们这些学生以为我还有什么隐瞒吗? 我是没有任何隐瞒的。我没有任何不可以向你们公开的,这就是我孔丘的为人。"

Confucius said, "My disciples, do you think that I have any secrets? I have no secrets from you. It is my way to do nothing without communicating it to you. That is what I am."

子曰:"巧言、令色、足恭,左丘明耻之,丘亦耻之。匿怨而友其人,左丘明耻之,丘亦耻之。"

(《论语·公冶长》)

〔译文〕孔子说:"花言巧语,伪装和善,过分卑恭,左丘明认为可耻，我也认为可耻。内心隐藏着对人的怨恨而表面上装出友好的样子，左丘明认为可耻，我也认为可耻。"

Confucius said, "Zuo Qiuming was ashamed of clever talk, a pretentious manner and overdeference, and I am ashamed of them, too. He was also ashamed to act friendly toward a man while inwardly angry with him, and so am I."

子曰："后生可畏，焉知来者之不如今也？四十、五十而无闻焉，斯亦不足畏也矣。"

(《论语·子罕》)

〔译文〕孔子说："年轻人是可敬畏的，怎么知道他们将来不如现在我们这一辈呢？如果一个人到了四十岁，五十岁仍然默默无闻，也就没有什么可敬畏的了。"

Confucius said, "Juniors are to be revered. How do you know that they will not be our equals in the future ? If at forty or fifty, however, they have achieved no reputation, they need no longer be revered."

孟子曰："饥者甘食，渴者甘饮，是未得饮食之正也，饥渴害之也。岂惟口腹有饥渴之害？人心亦皆有害。人能无以饥渴之害为心害，则不及人不为忧矣。"

（《孟子·尽心上》）

〔译文〕孟子说："饥饿的人吃起什么食物来都觉着甘甜，干渴的人喝起什么饮料来也都觉着甘甜，这是因为特别饥渴，而不知道食品、饮料正常的滋味。难道只有口舌肚皮才会受到饥渴的损害吗？人心也会受到这样的损害。如果人心不受到这种损害的话，那就不会因为赶不上别人而忧虑了。"

Mencius said, "A hungry person eats every kind of food deliciously and a thirsty person drinks every kind of beverage sweetly, this is because hunger and thirst impair the appetite and make these persons know not the original tastes of food and beverage. Could it be said that only the mouth and the stomach can be impaired by hunger and thirst? The heart would be also similarly impaired. If one often cultivates one's virtue and is able to make one's heart not impaired in the same way, one would not be worried because one is not equal to others."

子曰："躬自厚而薄责于人，则远怨矣。"

（《论语·卫灵公》）

〔译文〕孔子说："多责备自己而少责备别人，那么就可远远地避开怨恨了。"

Confucius said, "If a man demands much from himself and

little from others, he will certainly keep away resentments. "

子曰:"不患无位,患所以立。不患莫己知,求为可知也。"

(《论语·里仁》)

〔译文〕孔子说:"不愁没有职位,就愁没有任职的本领。不愁别人不知道自己,只求自己有值得别人知道的事情。"

Confucius said, "Don't mind not being in office, but rather mind whether one has qualities that entitle him to office. Don't mind that no one knows of you, but rather seek to be worth knowing. "

孟子曰:"自暴者,不可与有言也;自弃者,不可与有为也。"

(《孟子·离娄上》)

〔译文〕孟子说:"自己伤害自己的人,不能和他谈出有价值的言语;自己抛弃自己的人,不能和他做出有价值的事情。"

Mencius said, "We can not talk valuable words with those who cruelly injure themselves; we can not go in for a valuable cause with those who have no responsibility for themselves at all. "

子曰:"不曰'如之何,如之何'者,吾未如之何也已矣。"

（《论语·卫灵公》）

〔译文〕孔子说:"遇事不说'怎么办、怎么办'的人,我对这种人也不知道怎么办了。"

Confucius said, "If a man does not repeatedly ask himself 'What am I to do about it?' there is no possibility of my doing anything about him."

孟子曰:"可以取,可以无取,取伤廉;可以与,可以无与,与伤惠;可以死,可以无死,死伤勇。"

（《孟子·离娄下》）

〔译文〕孟子说:"可拿,可不拿,拿了对廉洁有伤害;可给,可不给,给了对恩惠有损害;可死,可不死,死了对勇敢有损害。"

Mencius said, "When you may take or you may not, it will do harm to your honest reputation to take. When you may give or you may not, it will do harm to your favour to give. When you may die or you may not, it will do harm to bravery to die."

孟子曰:"非其道,则一箪食不可受於人;如其道,则舜受尧之天下,不以为泰一子以为泰乎?"

(《孟子·滕文公下》)

〔译文〕孟子说:"如果不合理,就是一筐饭都不可以接受;如果合理,舜接受了尧的天下,也不以为过分——你以为过分了吗?"

Mencius said,"If it is unrational,you should not accept it even if it is a basketful of food；If rational,it is not excessive that King Shun accepted the kingdom of King Yao – Do you think it is excessive?"

子曰:"……过,则无惮改。"

(《论语·学而》)

〔译文〕孔子说:"……有了过错,就不要害怕改正。"

Confucius said,"If you have done wrong,be not ashamed to make amends."

孟子曰:"人恒过,然后能改;困于心,衡于虑,而后作;征于色,发于声,而后喻。入则无法家拂士,出则无敌国外患者,国恒亡。然后知生于忧患而死于安乐也。"

(《孟子·告子下》)

〔译文〕孟子说:"一个人,错误常常发生,才能改正;心意困苦,思虑阻塞,才能振作起来。表现在面色上,吐发在言语中,才能被人了解。一个国家内部没有讲法度的人相辅佐,外部没有敌国外患的忧虑,经常容易被灭亡。这样就可以知道忧愁患害能使人生存,安逸快乐能使人死亡的道理了。"

Mencius said, "A person can correct himself after making faults; he can only bestir himself after deep distress and the clogging of pondering; he can only be understood by expressing himself in facial expressions or in words. A state will die out if it has neither men knowing laws to assist at home, nor worries of aggression from abroad. Thus we may understand the truth that worry and disaster can make people survive while comfort and happiness can make people die."

子曰:"过而不改,是谓过矣。"

(《论语·卫灵公》)

〔译文〕孔子说:"犯了错误而不肯改正,这才叫做真正的过错呢。"

Confucius said, "The real fault is to have faults and not try to amend them."

孟子曰:"今有人日攘其邻之鸡者,或告之曰:'是非君子之道。'曰:'请损之,月攘一鸡,以待来年,然后已。'——如知其非义,斯速已矣,何待来年?"

(《孟子·滕文公下》)

〔译文〕孟子说:"现在有一个人,每天偷邻居家一只鸡,有人忠告他:'这不是君子干的事。'他说:'我要减少这种行为,那就一个月偷一只吧。等到明年,我就不偷了。'——如果知道这是一种不义的行为,便赶快停止算了,为什么要等到明年呢?"

Mencius said, "There is a person who steals one chicken from his neighbours everyday. Someone admonishes him, 'This is not the thing a gentleman does.' He says, 'I want to reduce this kind of behaviour, I may steal one every month then. I well stop stealing by next year,'—If he knows that this is not a just behaviour, he should simply stop it right now; why does he have to wait till next year?"

孟子曰:"西子蒙不洁,则人皆掩鼻而过之;虽有恶人,斋戒沐浴,则可以祀上帝。"

(《孟子·离娄下》)

〔译文〕孟子说:"如果西施身上沾染了肮脏,别人走过她身边时也会掩着鼻子;既使是面貌丑陋的人,如果他斋戒沐浴,也一样可以祭祀上帝。"

Mencius said, "If the beautiful lady Xishi has something dirty on her clothes, others would pass by holding their noses. Even though a person's features are ugly, he may offer sacrifices to God after fast and ablution."

孟子曰:"说大人,则藐之,勿视其巍巍然。"

(《孟子·尽心下》)

〔译文〕孟子说:"向诸侯进言,就得轻视他。不要把他高高在上的地位放在眼里。"

Mencius said, "When urging a duke to adopt your political views, you must look down upon him to strengthen your own confidence. Do not think too much of his high position."

子贡问:"师与商也孰贤?"子曰:"师也过,商也不及。"曰:"然则师愈与?"子曰:"过犹不及。"

(《论语·先进》)

〔译文〕子贡问孔子："颛孙师与卜商,哪一个人更好些呢?"孔子说:"颛孙师做起事来,常常过分;而卜商做起来,却又常常不到火候。"子贡接着又问:"那么,是不是可以说颛孙师比卜商好一些呢?"孔子说:"不是的,事情做过了头与做不到是一样的。"

Zi Gong asked, "Who is the better, Shi or Shang?" Confucius said, "Shi often goes too far and Shang does not go far enough." Zi Gong said, "In that case, Shi must be the better?" Confucius said, "To go too far is as bad as not to go far enough."

子张学干禄。子曰:"多闻阙疑,慎言其余,则寡尤;多见阙殆,慎行其余,则寡悔。言寡尤,行寡悔,禄在其中矣。"

(《论语·为政》)

〔译文〕子张向孔子学求官职得俸禄的方法。孔子说:"多听,有怀疑的问题,加以保留,其余有把握的部分,谨慎地说出自己的看法,这样就可以少犯错误。多看,有疑惑不清的事情,暂时搁下,其余有把握的,谨慎地去实行,那么就能减少后悔。言语错误少,行动懊悔少,官职俸禄就在其中了。"

Zi Zhang asked for a view to high rank and good pay. Confucius said, "Hear much, but maintain silence as regards doubtful points and be cautious in speaking the rest; then you will seldom fall into error. See much, but maintain silence as regards what is doubtful and be cautious in acting upon the rest; then you will seldom have repentance. He who seldom errors in speech or repents his actions will surely be rewarded with high rank and good pay."

子曰:"弟子,入则孝,出则悌,谨而信,泛爱众,而亲仁。行有余力,则以学文。"

(《论语·学而》)

[译文]孔子说:"少年子弟回到家里要孝顺父母,外出要敬爱兄长,做事要谨慎小心,说话要讲究信用,要广泛爱护大众而亲近有仁德的人。这样做了之后还有多余的精力,就要用来学习文化知识。"

Confucius said, "A young man should behave well to his parents at home and to his elders out of doors. He should be cautious but truthful. He should have charity in his heart for all men, but seek the intimacy of the virtuous. If, when all that is done, he has an energy to spare, then let him study literary culture."

樊迟问知。子曰:"务民之义,敬鬼神而远之,可谓知矣。"

(《论语·雍也》)

〔译文〕樊迟问怎样才算聪明,孔子说:"专心致力于人民认为合理的事情,尊敬鬼神却远离它,可以算得聪明了。"

Fan Chi asked about wisdom. Confucius said, "The man who devotes himself to what the common people think is just and right, who respects the spirits but keeps them at a distance, may be termed wise."

子曰:"攻乎异端,斯害也已。"

(《论语·为政》)

〔译文〕孔子说:"一心去攻读钻研异端邪说,这就是祸害啊。"

Confucius said, "It is indeed harmful to set one´s mind upon utterly new and strange doctrines."

季文子三思而后行。子闻之,曰:"再,斯可矣。"

(《论语·公冶长》)

〔译文〕季文子每件事考虑多次才行动。孔子听后说:"考虑两次,也就可以了。"

Ji Wenzi acted only after thinking thrice. On hearing of this, Confucius said, "Twice is quite enough."

子曰："法语之言，能无从乎？改之为贵。巽与之言，能无说乎？绎之为贵。说而不绎，从而不改，吾未知之何也已矣。"

（《论语·子罕》）

〔译文〕孔子说："合乎法典、法规的话，能够不听从吗？但听从之后要改正错误才可贵。谦恭顺耳的话，听了能够不高兴吗？但要对这些话分析鉴别才可贵。只高兴而不分析鉴别，只听从而不改正错误，对这种人我实在是没有办法啊。"

Confucius said, "The codes must be followed, but the important thing is self-reformation. The obedient and flattering words are pleasing, but the important thing is analysis and identification. For those who approve but do not analyze, who accept but do not change, I can do nothing at all."

子曰："居上不宽，为礼不敬，临丧不哀，吾何以观之哉？"

（《论语·八佾》）

〔译文〕孔子说："居于统治地位不宽宏大量，行礼的时候不恭敬严肃，参加丧礼的时候不悲哀，这种样子，我怎么能看得下去呢？"

Confucius said, "High office filled by men of narrow views, ceremonious act performed without reverence, the forms of mourning observed without grief – these are things I cannot bear to see!"

子曰:"德之不修,学之不讲,闻义不能徙,不善不能改,是吾忧也。"

(《论语·述而》)

〔译文〕孔子说:"对自己的品德不培养,学过的东西不讲习,明明听到义在那里,却不能亲身赴之,明明知道自己有缺点错误,却不能改正,这些都是我所忧虑的啊!"

Confucius said, "Not to improve one's moral characters, not to review all that one has learned, not to approach what is righteous though knowing where it is, not to rectify one's faults – these are my worries."

子曰:"诵诗三百,授之以政,不达;使于四方,不能专对;虽多,亦奚以为。"

(《论语·子路》)

〔译文〕孔子说:"熟读了《诗经》三百篇,叫他去处理政务,却行不通；派他出使外国，又不能独立地谈判应酬；读得虽多，又有什么用处呢？"

Confucius said, "A man may be able to recite all three hundred of The Poems, but when he is given a position in the government he is unsuccessful, or when sent on a mission to foreign countries, he proves unable to think for himself and manage. Even though he may know many poems, of what use is it to him?"

子曰："非其鬼而祭之，谄也。见义不为，无勇也。"

（《论语·为政》）

[译文]孔子说："祭祀自己不应该祭祀的鬼神，是献媚。见到应该挺身而出的事却袖手旁观，是怯懦。"

Confucius said, "It is flattery to offer sacrifices to the dead who do not belong to your own family. It is cowardice to fail to do what is just."

孟子曰："于不可已而已者，无所不已。于所厚者薄，无所不薄也。其进锐者，其退速。"

（《孟子·尽心上》）

〔译文〕孟子说:"对于不该停止的工作却停止了,那就没有什么不可以停止的了。对于该厚待的人却去薄待他,那也就没有谁不可以薄待的了。前进太猛的人,后退也会快。"

Mencius said, "If one stops the work that should not be stopped, there is nothing that can not be stopped. If one unkindly treats the person who should be treated kindly, there is nobody who can not be treated unkindly. Those who make too fiece and sudden progress would also retreat quickly."

冉求曰:"非不说子之道,力不足也。"子曰:"力不足者,中道而废。今女画。"

(《论语·雍也》)

〔译文〕冉求说:"不是我不喜欢您的学说,是我力量不够。"孔子说:"能力不够的人,是走到中途走不动了才停止。现在你是先划一个界限而止步不前。"

Ran Qiu said, "It isn't that I dislike the Master's doctrine. It's just that I haven't enough energy to follow it." Confucius said, "One who hasn't enough energy becomes collapsed during the course of the journey, but yours is a case of deliberate choice."

子曰:"譬如为山,未成一篑,止,吾止也。譬如平地,虽复一篑,进,吾往也。"

(《论语·子罕》)

〔译文〕孔子说:"比方用土堆山,只要再加一筐土,便可堆成了,如果停下来,那是我自己要停下来的。又比方用土平地,即使刚刚倒下第一筐土,如果前进,那也是我自己要前进的。"

Confucius said, "Though in making a mound I should stop when one basketful of earth would complete it, it is because I wanted to stop. On the other hand, if in leveling land I advanced my work by but one basketful, it is because I wanted to advance myself. "

孟子曰:"言人之不善,当如后患何?"

(《孟子·离娄下》)

〔译文〕孟子说:"宣扬别人的不好,出现了后患该怎么办呢?"

Mencius said, "If you speak ill of others, how will you do with the future troubles?"

子曰："士志于道,而耻恶衣恶食者,未足与议也。"

（《论语·里仁》）

〔译文〕孔子说："读书人有志于追求真理,但又以自己吃粗粮、穿破衣服为耻辱,这种人是不值得与他们谈论真理的。"

Confucius said, "I can not discuss things with a learner whose heart is set upon the truth, but who is at the same time ashamed of poor clothes and bad food."

子曰："群居终日,言不及义,好行小慧,难矣哉!"

（《论语·卫灵公》）

〔译文〕孔子说："整天聚集在一起,说话不合道理,喜欢卖弄小聪明,这种人是很难教育的呀!"

Confucius said, "Those who spend a whole day together without speaking any words of reason but petty clever talks are indeed difficult to educate."

孟子曰："祸福无不自己求之者。"

（《孟子·公孙丑上》）

〔译文〕孟子说："祸害或者幸福没有不是自己找来的。"

Mencius said, "Disaster or happiness will befall upon one just because he seeks it."

孟子曰："饥者易为食,渴者易为饮。"

　　　　　　　　　　　《孟子·公孙丑上》

〔译文〕孟子说："肚子饥饿的人不苟择食物,口干舌燥的人不苟择饮料。"

Mencius said, "A hungry man does not choose food, nor does a thirsty man choose drinks."

万章问曰："敢问交际何心也?"
孟子曰："恭也。"

　　　　　　　　　　　《孟子·万章下》

〔译文〕万章问道："请问交际的时候,应该抱有什么心情?"
孟子答道："应该抱着恭敬的心情。"

Wan Zhang asked Mencius, "Would you tell me what feeling I should have when I communicate with others?"
Mencius answered, "The feeling of respect."

子曰:"益者三友,损者三友。友直、友谅、友多闻,益矣;友便辟、友善柔、友便佞,损矣。"

（《论语·季氏》）

〔译文〕孔子说:"有益的朋友有三种,有害的朋友也有三种。与正直的人交朋友,与诚实的人交朋友,与见闻广博的人交朋友,便可得到好处。与谄媚奉承的人交朋友,与明一套暗一套的人交朋友,与夸夸其谈的人交朋友,便有害了。"

Confucius said, "There are three types of friends that are profitable and three types that are harmful. Friendship with the upright, the devoted and the learned is profitable; while friendship with the flattering, the double-faced and the too eloquent is harmful."

万章问曰:"敢问友。"

孟子曰:"不挟长,不挟贵,不挟兄弟而友。友也者,友其德也,不可以有挟也。"

（《孟子·万章下》）

〔译文〕万章问道:"请问怎样交朋友。"

孟子说:"不倚仗自己年纪大,不仗恃自己地位高,不倚仗自己兄弟的富贵。交朋友,是因为朋友的品德好才去交他,心中不要存在有任何倚仗的观念。"

Wan Zhang asked, "Please tell me how to make friends."
Mencius said, "Do not rely on your old age, your high position or your brothers' wealth. You make a friend with someone because he has good moral character; do not have any sense of reliance in your mind."

　　子贡问友。子曰:"忠告而善道之,不可则止,毋自辱焉。"
　　　　　　　　　　　　　　　　　　　(《论语·颜渊》)

　　〔译文〕子贡问怎样对待朋友,孔子说:"忠心地劝告他,好好地引导他,他不听从,也就罢了,不要自找侮辱。"

Zi Gong asked about friends, Confucius said, "In all loyalty point out their good and bad points, be skillful in guiding them. If they disapprove, desist, Don't go so far as to court humiliation."

　　孟子谓万章曰:"一乡之善士斯友一乡之善士,一国之善士斯友一国之善士,天下之善士斯友天下之善士。以友天下之善士为未足,又尚论古之人。颂其诗,读其书,不知其人,可乎? 是以论其世也。是尚友也。"
　　　　　　　　　　　　　　　　　　　(《孟子·万章下》)

〔译文〕孟子对万章说:"一个乡村的优秀人物便和那一乡村的优秀人物交朋友,一个国家的优秀人物便和那个国家的优秀人物交朋友,天下的优秀人物便和天下的优秀人物交朋友。如果认为结交天下的优秀人物做朋友还不够,还要向前去找古时的优秀人物。吟咏他们作的诗,读他们写的书,不了解他的为人,可以吗? 所以要讨论他那个时代。这就是追溯历史与古人交朋友。"

Mencius said to Wan Zhang, "The outstanding people in a village should make friends with the outstanding people in the village. The outstanding people in a country should make friends with the outstanding people in the country. The outstanding people in the world should make friends with the outstanding people in the world. If that is still not enough, we should find the outstanding people in ancient times. We can read their poems and books. How can it be all right to make friend with somebody without knowing how he behaves himself in society? So we should discuss the ancient times. This is the so - called tracing history to make friends with the ancient people."

朋友死,无所归。曰:"由我殡。"

《论语·乡党》

〔译文〕朋友死了，没人管。孔子说：“由我来负责办理丧事。”

When a friend died and there were no relatives to make arrangements for the funeral, Confucius said, "Let me take up the services."

子曰：“始吾于人也，听其言而信其行；今吾于人也，听其言而观其行……。"

（《论语·公冶长》）

〔译文〕孔子说：“以前我和别人交往时，听到他的话，便相信他的行为。今天我和别人交往时，我不但要听他说的话，还要考察一下他的行为……。"

Confucius said, "At first, my way of dealing with others was to listen to their words and to take their actions upon trust. Now, my way is to listen to what they say and then watch to see what they do."

子曰：“不得中行而与之，必也狂狷乎！狂者进取，狷者有所不为也。"

（《论语·子路》）

〔译文〕孔子说:"我找不到言行合乎中庸的人而和他们交往,那一定要交激进的人和狷介的人吧! 激进的人勇于进取,狷介的人不做坏事。"

Confucius said, "If I can't find moderate men to deal with, I must turn to the impetuous and upright. The former will always progress and the latter will not do bad things."

子路问曰:"何如斯可谓之士矣?"子曰:"切切偲偲,怡怡如也,可谓士矣。朋友切切偲偲,兄弟怡怡。"

(《论语·子路》)

〔译文〕子路问道:"怎样才可以叫做士呢?"孔子说:"互相勉励,亲切和气,可以叫做士了。朋友之间互相勉励,兄弟之间亲切和气。"

Zi Lu asked, "What must a man be like to merit the title of gentleman?" Confucius said, "He must be critical and sincere, kind and accommodating. Be critical and sincere with regard to the conduct of his friends; be kind and accommodating towards his brothers."

子谓颜渊曰:"用之则行,舍之则藏,惟我与尔有是夫!"
子路曰:"子行三军,则谁与?"

子曰:"暴虎冯河,死而无悔者,吾不与也。必也临事而惧,好谋而成者也。"

(《论语·述而》)

[译文]孔子对颜渊说:"用我呢,就干起来,不用呢,就藏起来,只有我和你才能这样吧!"

子路说:"您如果率领军队,愿同谁共事呢?"

孔子说:"赤手空拳和老虎搏斗,不用船只去渡河,这样死了都不后悔的人,我是不和他共事的。同我共事的一定要遇事谨慎小心,善于谋略而能完成任务的人。"

Confucius said to Yan Hui, "The maxim

When wanted, then go to work;

When set aside, then live quietly

Is one that you and I could certainly fulfil. " Zi Lu then asked, "If you were in charge of the army, whom would you take with you?" Confucius said, "I would not take along one who was ready to 'beard a tiger or rush a river' without caring whether he lived or died. I should certainly take someone who approached difficulties with caution and who preferred to succeed by strategy. "

子曰:"视其所以,观其所由,察其所安。人焉廋哉? 人焉廋哉?"

(《论语·为政》)

〔译文〕孔子说："看一个人为人做事的目的,观察他为达到一定目的所用的方式方法,了解他安于什么,不安于什么。那么,这个人到底如何怎么能隐蔽得了呢? 到底怎么能隐蔽得了呢?"

Confucius said, "Look closely into one's aims, observe the means by which he pursues them and discover what brings him content. And then can the man's real worth remain hidden from you, can it remain hidden from you?"

孟子曰:"存乎人者,莫良于眸子。眸子不能掩其恶。胸中正,则眸子瞭焉;胸中不正,则眸子眊焉。听其言也,观其眸子,人焉廋哉?"

(《孟子·离娄上》)

〔译文〕孟子说:"观察一个人,最好是观察他的眼睛。因为眼睛不能遮盖一个人的丑恶。心正,眼就明亮;心不正,眼就昏暗。听一个人说话的时候,注意观察他的眼睛,这个人的善恶又能往哪里隐藏呢?"

Mencius said, "When you observe a person, the best way is to observe his eyes, as eyes can not hide the person's evils. His eyes will be bright if he has no evil intentions; his eyes will be dim if he harbors evil intentions. When you listen to a person speak, just look at his eyes his goodness or evil will be displayed there."

子曰："众恶之,必察焉;众好之,必察焉。"

（《论语·卫灵公》）

〔译文〕孔子说："大家都讨厌他,一定要考察一下原因;大家都喜欢他,也一定要考察一下原因。"

Confucius said, "When everyone dislikes a man, enquiry is necessary; when everyone likes a man, enquiry is also necessary."

子贡问曰："乡人皆好之,何如?"子曰："未可也。"

"乡人皆恶之,何如?"子曰："未可也。不如乡人之善者好之,其不善者恶之。

（《论语·子路》）

〔译文〕子贡问道："家乡里人都喜欢他,这个人怎么样?"孔子说："还不行。"子贡又问道："家乡里人都厌恶他,这个人怎么样?"孔子说："还不行。最好是全乡的好人都喜欢他,全乡的坏人都厌恶他。"

Zi Gong asked, "What would you think of a man who is

liked by all his fellow – villagers?" Confucias said, "That is not enough." Zi Gong asked again, "What would you think of a man who is disliked by all his fellow – villagers?" Confucius said, "That is not enough. Best of all would be that the good people in his village all like him and the bad all dislike him."

孔子曰:"……不知言,无以知人也。"

(《论语·尧曰》)

〔译文〕孔子说:"……不懂得分辨人家的言语,就不可能了解人。"

Confucius said, "He who does not understand words, cannot understand people."

公孙丑曰:"何谓知言?"

孟子曰:"诐辞知其所蔽,淫辞知其所陷,邪辞知其所离,遁辞知其所穷。"

(《孟子·公孙丑上》)

〔译文〕公孙丑问:"怎么样才算善于分析别人的言辞呢?"

孟子回答说:"不全面的言词我知道它片面在何处,过份的言词我知道它的缺陷在何处,不正当的话我知道它与正当话的分歧在何处,躲躲闪闪的言词我知道它理屈在何处。"

Gongsun Chou asked,"How do you have a sound analysis of other's words?"

Mencius answered, "I'll try to learn where are the lopsideness in incomplete words, the limit in excessive words, the wrongness in incorrect words, and the inability to advance any further arguments for justification in subterfuge."

子曰:"可与言而不与之言,失人;不可与言而与之言,失言。知者不失人,亦不失言。"

(《论语·卫灵公》)

〔译文〕孔子说:"可以同他谈话,而不同他谈,这是错过人才;不可以同他谈话,而同他谈,这是浪费言语。聪明人不错过人才,也不浪费言语。"

Confucius said,"Not to talk to one who can be talked to, is to lose a man; to talk to one who can not be talked to, is to waste words. The wise never lose men, nor do they waste words."

"唐棣之华,偏其反而。岂不尔思? 室是远而。"子曰:"未之思也,夫何远之有?"

(《论语·子罕》)

〔译文〕古诗写道:"唐棣树的花呀,翩翩地摇摆着,难道我不想念你? 只是住处相隔太遥远。"孔子说:"他并没有真的去想念哩,如果真的想念,还怕什么遥远吗?"

An ancient poem read, "As the flowers of the wild cherry tree flutter and turn, couldn't I help but think of you? Yet your house is far from here." Confucius said, "He did not really love her. Had he done so, he would not have worried about the distance."

子曰:"不患人之不己知,患不知人也。"

(《论语·学而》)

〔译文〕孔子说:"不要担忧别人不了解自己,应该忧虑的倒是自己不了解别人。"

Confucius said, "I am not concerned that other men do not know me; I am concerned that I do not know other men."

孝悌篇第六

BOOK Ⅵ FILIAL PIETY

孟懿子问孝。子曰:"无违。"

樊迟御,子告之曰:"孟孙问孝于我,我对曰:'无违。'"樊迟曰:"何谓也?"子曰:"生,事之以礼;死,葬之以礼,祭之以礼。"

(《论语·为政》)

〔译文〕孟懿子问什么是孝。孔子说:"不要违背礼节。"樊迟给孔子赶车,孔子告诉樊迟说:"孟孙向我问孝,我答复他说,不要违背礼节。"樊迟说:"你说的是什么意思呢?"孔子说:"父母活着时,按照礼节侍奉他们;死了,按照礼节埋葬他们,祭祀他们。"

Meng Yizi asked about filial duty. "Don't go against the rites," Confucius replied. Later when Fan Chi was driving carriage for him, Confucius said to Fan, "Meng asked about filial duty and I said 'Don't go against the rites.'" "What did you mean by that?" asked Fan. Confucius said, "While the parents live, serve them according to the rites. When they die, bury them and make the offerings to them according to the rites."

孟子曰:"大孝终身慕父母。五十而慕者,予於大舜见之矣。"

(《孟子·万章上》)

〔译文〕孟子说:"只有最孝顺的人才终身怀恋父母。到了五十岁还怀恋父母的,我在伟大的舜身上见到了。"

Mencius said, "Only the most filial people will think of their parents fondly and all their lives. I saw this in the great Shun. He still thought fondly of his parents when reaching the age of fifty."

孟子曰:"亲丧,固所自尽也。"

(《孟子·滕文公上》)

〔译文〕孟子说:"父母的丧事,本应该自动地尽心竭力的。"

Mencius said, "One should manage his parents' funeral voluntarily and with all his efforts."

子夏问孝。子曰:"色难。有事,弟子服其劳;有酒食,先生馔,曾是以为孝乎?"

(《论语·为政》)

〔译文〕子夏问什么是孝。孔子说:"侍奉父母经常做到和颜悦色很难。有事情,儿子替父母效劳;有好酒好菜,让父母吃喝;难道这竟可认为是孝吗?"

Zi Xia asked about filial duty. Confucius said, "It's difficult for a son to have a pleasant facial expression all the time. The youngsters undertake the hard work when anything has to be done, or serve their elders first with wine and food. But can this be called filial piety?"

子游问孝。子曰:"今之孝者,是谓能养。至于犬马,皆能有养。不敬,何以别乎?"

(《论语·为政》)

〔译文〕子游问什么是孝。孔子说:"现在的所谓孝,似乎能养活父母就行了。就是狗马,都能得到饲养。如果内心对父母没有孝敬之情,那供养父母和饲养狗马有什么区别呢?"

Zi You asked about filial duty. Confucius said, "Filial sons nowadays are those who merely get enough food for their parents. But even dogs and horses are cared for to that extent. If they don't show respect for their parents, where lies the difference between parents and animals in it?"

孟子曰："吾闻之也:君子不以天下俭其亲。"

(《孟子·公孙丑》)

〔译文〕孟子说:"我听说过:君子在任何情况下都不在父母身上去省钱。"

Mencius said, "I heard tlat a gentleman will never save money on his parents."

孟子曰："父母爱之,喜而不忘;父母恶之,劳而不怨。"

(《孟子·万章上》)

〔译文〕孟子曾说:"父母喜爱时,虽然高兴,却不因此而懈怠;父母厌恶时,虽然忧愁,却不因此而怨恨。"

Mencius said, "When parents love you, you are happy, but you shouldn't become lazy; when parents dislike you, you become worried, but you should not bear a grudge against them."

孟子曰："食而弗爱,豕交之也;爱而不敬,兽畜之也。恭敬者,币之未将者也。恭敬而无实,君子不可虚拘。"

(《孟子·尽心上》)

〔译文〕孟子说:"对于人只养活,而不爱,等于养猪;只是爱,而不尊敬,等于豢养狗马。恭敬之心,应该是在向别人奉送礼物之前就有了。不可以只有恭敬的形式,而没有恭敬的实质。一个有道德的人,不可以被这种虚假的礼节所束缚。"

Mencius said, "For a man, if you just feed him, but do not love him, that's just as if you feed a pig. Furthermore, if you love him, but do not respect him, that's just as if you feed a dog or a horse. You should cherish a feeling of reverence before you present a gift to somebody. It's no good to have the form of reverence but no content of it. A virtuous man shouldn't be restrained by this false etiquette."

孟武伯问孝。子曰:"父母唯其疾之忧。"

(《论语·为政》)

〔译文〕孟武伯向孔子请教孝道。孔子说:"做父母的只是为孝子的疾病而忧愁。"

Meng Wubo asked about filial duty. Confucius said, "Behave in such a way that your parents have no worry and anxiety about you, except concerning your health."

宰我问:"三年之丧,期已久矣。君子三年不为礼,礼必

坏;三年不为乐,乐必崩。旧谷既没,新谷既升,钻燧改火,期
可已矣。"

子曰:"食夫稻,衣夫锦,于女安乎?"

曰:"安。"

"女安,则为之! 夫君子与居丧,食旨不甘,闻乐不乐,居
处不安,故不为也。今女安,则为之!"

宰我出,子曰:"予之不仁也! 子生三年,然后免于父母之
怀。夫三年之丧,天下之通丧也。予也有三年之爱于其父母
乎?"

(《论语·阳货》)

〔译文〕宰我问:"子女为父母服丧三年,为期也太久了。
君子有三年不去习礼仪,礼仪一定会败坏;三年不去奏音乐,
音乐一定会荒废。旧谷既已吃完了,新谷又已经登场,取火用
的木头也已改换了一遍,服丧一周年就可以了。"

孔子说:"(父母死了不满三年)你便吃那白米饭,穿那锦
缎衣,对你来说心安吗?"

宰我说:"心安。"

孔子说:"你心安,那么你就那样去干吧! 君子在服丧期
间,吃美味不感到香甜,听音乐不感到快乐,住在家里不感到
安适,所以不那样做。如今你既然感到心安,便去干好了。"

宰我退了出来。孔子说:"宰予真不仁呀! 儿女生下来,
三年后才能完全脱离父母的怀抱。为父母服丧三年,是天下
通行的丧礼呀。宰予难道就没有从他父母怀抱中得到过三年
爱抚吗?"

Zai Wo asked about the three years' mourning saying, "Three years' period of mourning is too long. If a gentleman suspends his practice of rites for three years, rites will certainly decay; if for three years he makes no music, music will certainly be destroyed. In a year the old crops have already vanished, the new crops have come up; woods for making fire have finished their round(woods for making fire change every season, the new fire is in each case kindled on the wood of a tree appropriate to the season). Surely a year's period of mourning would be enough."

Confucius said, "Would you then feel at ease in eating good rice and wearing silk brocades?"

Zai Wo said, "Quite at ease."

Confucius said, "If you would really feel at ease, then do so. But when a gentleman is in mourning, if he eats dainties, he does not relish them; if he hears music, it does not please him; if he lives in his normal resting place, he is not comfortable. Hence he abstains from these things. But if you would really feel at ease, then go and do them."

When Zai Wo had gone out, Confucius said, "How inhuman Zai Yu(i. e. Zai Wo)is! Only when a child is three years old does it leave its parents' arms. The three years' mourning is the universal mourning everywhere under Heaven. And Zai Yu-was he not loved dearly by his parents for three years?"

子曰："父在，观其志；父没，观其行；三年无改于父之道，可谓孝矣。"

（《论语·学而》）

〔译文〕孔子说："父亲在世时看他的志向；父亲逝世后看他的行为；如果三年之内不改变父亲留下的正确原则，就可以说他是孝子了。"

Confucius said, "While his father lives, observe a man's intentions; when the father dies, observe his actions. If for three years a man does not change from the ways of his father, he may be called filial. "

孟子曰："世俗所谓不孝者五：惰其四肢，不顾父母之养，一不孝也；博奕好欲酒，不顾父母之养，二不孝也；好货财，私妻子，不顾父母之养，三不孝也；从耳目之欲，以为父母戮，四不孝也；好勇斗狠，以危父母，五不孝也。"

（《孟子·离娄下》）

〔译文〕孟子说："一般人所谓不孝的事有五件：四肢懒惰，不管父母的生活，一不孝；好下棋、饮酒，不管父母的生活，二不孝；贪恋钱财，偏爱妻子儿女，不管父母的生活，三不孝；放纵耳目的欲望，使父母因此受到耻辱，四不孝；逞强好斗，危及父母，五不孝。"

Mencius said, "People often say that there are five cases of being not in accordance with filial piety. First, one is lazy, regardless of one's parents' living. Second, one is fond of playing chess and drinking wine, regardless of one's parents' living. Third, one clings to wealth and shows partiality for one's wife and children, regardless of one's parents' living. Fourth, one is indulged in sensuous desires, making one's parents suffer humiliation. Fifth, one is fond of showing one's valour and fighting with others, endangering one's parents."

子曰："事父母几谏,见志不从,又敬不违,劳而不怨。"

《论语·里仁》

[译文]孔子说:"事奉父母,看见他们有不对的地方,应该委婉地劝止。如果父母心里不愿听从,仍然要恭恭敬敬而不触犯他们,只有在心里忧愁,而不要怨恨。"

Confucius said, "In serving his parents a man may gently remonstrate with them when they are wrong. But if he sees that he has failed to dissuade them, he should resume an attitude of respect and not offend them; he may feel worried, but not resentful."

子曰："父母之年,不可不知也。一则以喜,一则以惧。"

（《论语·里仁》）

〔译文〕孔子说："父母的年龄不能不时时记在心里呀,一方面为他们长寿而高兴,一方面为他们的衰老而担忧。"

Confucius said, "The parents' ages must not be neglected. On the one hand, it is a source of joy, on the other hand, it is a source of dread."

子曰："出则事公卿,入则事父兄,丧事不敢不勉,不为酒困,何有于我哉?"

（《论语·子罕》）

〔译文〕孔子说："出外服事国君和大臣,在家服事父亲兄长。有丧事不敢不尽礼,不被酒所困扰。这些事我做到了哪些呢?"

Confucius said, "At court, to serve duly the prince and his ministers; and at home, one's father and brothers. As regards matters of mourning, to be conscious of no neglect, nor to be overcome with wine. To which of these can I make any claim?"

子曰："孝哉闵子骞! 人不间于其父母昆弟之言。"

（《论语》·先进）

〔**译文**〕孔子说:"闵子骞真是孝顺呀! 人们对于他父母兄弟夸奖他的话挑不出毛病来。"

Confucius said, "Min Ziqian could be called filial indeed! No one can pick faults with the praising words by his parents and brothers. "

孟子曰:"道在迩而求诸远,事在易而求诸难。人人亲其亲,长其长,而天下平。"

（《孟子·离娄上》）

〔**译文**〕孟子说:"道在近处却到远处去求,事情本来很容易却往难处去做。只要各人亲爱自己的双亲,尊敬自己的长辈,天下就太平了。"

Mencius said, "Why do you try to find the principle from a distant place while it is nearby? Why do you work things into difficulty while they can be done very easily? If each one loves one's parents and respects one's elders, the world will be peaceful. "

孔 孟 箴 言

汉英对照本

李天辰　编译

*

山东友谊出版社出版发行

（地址：济南经九路胜利大街 39 号　邮编：250001）

山东新华印刷厂临沂厂印刷

*

787×1092 毫米 32 开本 6.75 印张 130 千字

1998 年 11 月第 1 版　　1998 年 11 月第 1 次印刷

印数 1－7000

ISBN 7—80642—103—3

Z·25　　定价：8.00 元